HE KNOWS YOUR HEART

OTHER BOOKS BY TONI SORENSON BROWN:

Book of Mormon Heroes

Bible Heroes

TONI
SORENSON
BROWN

Covenant Communications, Inc.
Covenant

Cover painting, *The First Rose* © Carol P. Harding.

Published by Covenant Communications, Inc.
American Fork, Utah

Printed in Canada
First Printing: April 2003

10 09 08 07 06 05 04 03 10 9 8 7 6 5 4 3 2 1

ISBN 1-59156-233-3

For
Lillian Izola Bartholomew

TABLE OF CONTENTS

PROLOGUE

I sat on the front row of the BYU women's leadership conference listening to the speaker, then a member of the General Relief Society Presidency, deliver an eloquent speech on faith. At least I think it was on faith. I couldn't hear a word for the thundering of my heart. You see, I was set to speak next.

Me, follow one of the most popular and profound speakers in the Church?

No way.

No how.

Somebody had made a gargantuan mistake. Though I'd done my share of public speaking, this time was different. I was listed as the "humorous" speaker, but I didn't feel funny. I felt fraudulent. I could sense my self-confidence melting like candle wax. (Or was it something else dripping down the back of my neck?) I scanned the massive room for the nearest exit; it was ninety miles away. In those moments I suffered a sort of spiritual meltdown. I became the arch enemy of the little engine that could.

I think I can't. I think I can't. I think I can't.

That was my mantra as I silently engaged in a deadly little game Satan entices us to play—*Compare and Contrast*. You know the rules. Pick a target—any target—as long as she is a Latter-day Saint woman. We can never, no matter how many home and personal enrichment meetings we attend, measure up. It's a stupid mind game; I don't know why I play it—every time I do, I lose. Every single time. Any time we focus on our differences, distancing ourselves from each other, everyone loses. Still, there I was listing the disparaging comparisons between frumpy, boring me and regal Sister Saint Perfect who was standing at the pulpit, quoting scriptures like she had penned them herself.

She was smarter than me. A lot smarter. She could deliver a punch line and could pronounce the word *abominable* without spitting on the microphone. I couldn't even say Wilford Woodruff three times in a row without biting my own tongue. Her suit was nicer and newer than mine. She was thinner and taller than me. She quoted scriptures, chapter and verse. At that moment, I couldn't even recall who the Book of Mormon was named after. She came from a stalwart family of steady faith. I was raised extraordinarily anti-Mormon. She served in high, holy callings. I was head diaper-taker-outer for our ward nursery.

The list of distinctions continued to grow and my heart continued to pound. "I'm sorry, Father," I prayed silently, actually getting up and bumping my way down the aisle. "I can't do this. I know I said I'd do it, and I really am honored, but I can't—*I am not Sister . . .*"

Then came a voice into my mind, a voice that stopped me dead in my cowardly, retreating tracks. It did not patronize nor punish me, but did *pierce me to the very center.* With unmistakable clarity I heard the declaration, "I never asked you to be anyone except Toni Brown. I know you. I know your heart. Just be you."

In that instant my ludicrous game playing ended. The Lord knew my name! He knew my heart! He was aware of all my faults and frailties—and still, he needed *me!*

Since then I have come to know unequivocally that the Lord knows each of us. He knows our names. He knows our hearts. He is aware of our strengths and weaknesses. He can name our favorite colors and the weight listed on our driver's licenses. He knows us that well. He knows us even better than we know ourselves.

And not only does he know us, he needs us. The realization brought to mind Elder Neal A. Maxwell's oft-quoted insight, "God does not begin by asking us about our ability, but only about our availability, and if we then prove our dependability, he will increase our capability!" ("It's Service, Not Status, That Counts," *Ensign*, July 1975, 7).

I went ahead and made my presentation. It was very different from the previous speech. I spoke in my own voice of diverse experiences. In conclusion, we both shared the same testimony borne to us by the same Holy Ghost: that Jesus is the Christ, the Son of the living God. He knows us. He needs us. He loves us.

Months later a woman in Florida approached me. "I heard you speak at BYU."

I turned around, surprised that she was addressing me. The woman smiled and reached into her purse from which she pulled a set of small scriptures. She opened to a back page covered in handwriting. "Look. I took notes on your message. I refer to them whenever I get discouraged. Thanks for feeding me."

"*Feeding* you?"

She nodded. "When I got to that conference my spirit was starved. I was weak and weary, and I felt unworthy when I looked around and saw all of the righteous sisters who surrounded me. Then you admitted experiencing those same feelings of inadequacy."

"I suspect, at times, we all feel inadequate," I said, remembering the suffocating strength of those emotions.

The woman tucked away her scriptures. "Well, it was manna to my soul," she said. "I was famished, then each presenter offered something different and delicious. I feasted until my spirit was nourished. I felt like I'd eaten a balanced meal."

I have given a great deal of thought to that woman's insight. We all need manna to stave off our hunger, be it physical or spiritual—manna prepared and served by a variety of bakers with their own knack of kneading the dough and seasoning the bread. It is my hope that between the pages of this book, you will find manna to nourish you. The recipes are not all my own; they are ground from the grain of many women who know how to host a feast.

The gospel is not a smorgasbord of truths from which we can pick and choose; it is a banquet that never leaves us hungry or malnourished. The prophet Amos foresaw the hunger that would rack our time. "Behold, the days come, saith the Lord God, that I will send a famine in the land, not a famine of bread, nor a thirst for water, but of hearing the words of the Lord" (Amos 8:11).

Speaking of this spiritual famine, Elder Jeffrey R. Holland of the Quorum of Twelve Apostles says, "I declare that God has through His Only Begotten Son lifted the famine of which Amos spoke. I testify that the Lord Jesus Christ is the Bread of Life and a Well of Living Water springing up unto eternal life" ("He Hath Filled the Hungry With Good Things," *Ensign*, Nov. 1997, 65).

The Ultimate Host, whose very words are life, promises, "I am the bread of life: he that cometh to me shall never hunger; and he that believeth on me shall never thirst" (John 6:35).

Whether we recognize it or not, our sustenance depends on the manna we receive from the Master. He provides the ingredients, but it is up to us to prepare them and to share them. President Gordon B. Hinckley states, "Under the sacred and compelling trust we have as members of the Church of Jesus Christ, ours is a work of redemption, of lifting and saving those who need help. Ours is a task of raising the sights of those of our people who fail to realize the great potential that lies within them" ("What This Work Is All About," *Ensign*, Aug. 2002 6–7).

Great potential lies within all of us. This book is about seeking and finding that potential. It's about hope, happiness, and spiritual health.

No matter who we are, where we are, or what we have to offer, we are needed to build the Kingdom—one meal at a time. Am I my sister's keeper? Yes! It is up to us to succor our sisters. This book is my humble offering. My recipe for manna is not the same as Sister Saint Perfect's. It is not the same as yours. And isn't that wonderful?

I have prepared this meal with love and ask only that you come hungry. The manna on this menu costs nothing, and what hungry woman in her right mind would turn down free food when a famine is threatening the land?

CHAPTER ONE

Invitation to a Feast

Come unto me and ye shall partake of the fruit of the tree of life; yea, ye shall eat and drink of the bread and the waters of life freely.
—*Alma 5:34*

We live in a world of stark contrasts. While one nation battles obesity, another faces famine. Do you realize that more than twenty thousand people die each day from hunger? As women, it is not in our divine nature to stand by and allow anyone to go hungry.

When was the last time you were truly hungry? I don't mean the gnawing growl of Fast Sunday, but genuine hunger? Looking at me now, you would never suspect that there was a time I went without food. It wasn't for very long. I didn't fast forty days and forty nights, and I did not starve like children in third-world refugee camps. I was seven or eight years old. My father was dead and my mother was an alcoholic. I don't recall the exact circumstances that found me home alone, but for days I'd been in an empty house with empty cupboards. No food and no money. Why didn't I just run to the neighbors' for peanut butter and jelly? Because I knew that if the neighbors discovered I'd been left alone, they'd call Child Services and I'd be placed in another foster home—for me, a fate worse than starvation.

The fridge was bare. Even the orange cardboard box of baking soda was hollow. I gulped a lot of water and watched television, but most of the commercials were about food. I slept as much as I could. I learned to like the taste of toothpaste. Hunger buzzed and stung, bounced around my empty stomach like a trapped hornet. I returned to the cupboards. In the far shadow on one shelf, way back in a forgotten corner, I discovered a small pile of spilled elbow macaroni shells. I savored each curve of dry pasta like it was a chocolate candy kiss.

I don't remember when my mother came home. I don't recall my next real meal. I just remember sitting there on the green linoleum floor, eating dried elbow macaroni from the palm of my hand, happy because I'd never tasted anything so delicious.

The gospel of Jesus Christ is delicious. Alma affirms, "the word is good, for it beginneth to enlarge my soul; yea, it beginneth to enlighten my understanding, yea, it beginneth to be delicious to me" (Alma 32:28).

Hunger has always been a motivator for God's children. Esau sold his birthright for a bowl of Cream of Wheat. Joseph's estranged and famished family was led to Egypt in search of grain. It was an empty stomach that ultimately made the prophet Lehi murmur against the Lord. Even Satan waited until Jesus was "an hungered" before he attempted to tempt the Son of Man.

My experience was minimal, but it gave me significant insight into Lehi's teaching: "it must needs be, that there is an opposition in all things"(2 Ne. 2:11). Opposition is a powerful teacher. How can we know that sweet is better until we've tasted the bitter? Hunger is bitter. It makes us humble. Famine has a way of speedily restoring faith. We fast to remind us that our very existence is reliant on the Lord's generous outpouring of life-giving and life-sustaining manna.

The next time I experienced genuine hunger it was not a physical longing; it was much more intense. My hunger was spiritual—I was in desperate need of heavenly manna. I had just become a first-time mother, the one blessing I had wanted more than anything. My joy and gratitude were overwhelming, and a new love stretched my Grinchy heart more than three sizes that day. I had expected those emotions. But no one warned me that in the midst of those initial bonding moments, a horrifying fear stalks new mothers, especially first-timers.

I felt inadequate, afraid, flattened by an unfamiliar and frightening emptiness that hit me like a semi-load of Idaho spuds. I was suddenly responsible for another life. Me, who for months had not even watered my houseplants.

Motherhood is noble. Lofty. The holiest station a woman can achieve, a partnership with the Almighty. "Before the world was created, in heavenly councils the pattern and role of women were prescribed. [We] were elected by God to be wives and mothers in

Zion. Exaltation in the celestial kingdom is predicated on faithfulness to that calling" (Ezra Taft Benson, "The Honored Place of Woman," *Ensign*, Nov. 1981, 104).

The baby that slept in my arms was fresh from the Father's presence. I looked at her carefully; she resembled Brigham Young without the beard. Still, I would have given my life to protect her. It was the power of that love that terrified me. We live in a world where the innocent and pure are the adversary's targets. How could I protect my baby from harm, from evil?

I should have cried out in prayer, "Help me!" I should have called my husband and poured out my heart. I should have run to the temple. Instead, I listened to a chorus of self-doubts orchestrated by the one who conducts all of our self-defeating thoughts. I believed the taunting whisper that I would have to fly solo in my parental responsibilities—a feat at which I was sure to fail. It was my singular duty to mold and protect my helpless babe. Momentarily, I forgot everything I knew about Heavenly Parents and the Plan of Salvation. I felt weak and incapable—literally starved for help. How was I supposed to care for my infant daughter? I couldn't even keep a houseplant alive. And she was no philodendron. This precious little miracle had a beating heart, flailing arms, legs, and a toothless mouth that gaped open like an unexpected black hole. Out came a wail that peeled the paint from the hospital walls.

Fear took on a new face. Reality dug in with both teensy, pink, wrinkled feet. The eight-pound bundle that struggled in my arms might as well have weighed eight thousand pounds. The weight of responsibility I felt was crushing. My daughter's needs were my needs. Her hunger made my stomach rumble. Her cries made tears trickle down my cheeks.

How could someone I'd only met moments before alter my life and change my heart so cataclysmically? President David O. McKay warned that being parents is "the greatest trust that has been given to human beings" (*The Responsibility of Parents to Their Children*, pamphlet, 1). He also said, "I believe a competent mother in every home is the greatest need in the world today" (*Words for Women*, 93).

About the only thing I wasn't feeling was competent.

Not only was it my duty to meet this child's physical needs and to protect her from the ghouls of hell, but I was responsible for her eternal salvation. Right then, I couldn't even remember what we had named her.

My baby was doomed.

What was a mother to do?

"Feed her," said the nurse who rushed into the room, summoned by my daughter's piercing screams.

Of course, my baby was crying because she was hungry. What kind of mother was I to miss such an obvious sign? I pressed her little body to mine. Her diaper needed changing as well. My arms extended the tiny pink bundle out to the nurse. "I'm the worst mother in the world," I confessed.

The woman declined my offer. She just stood by my bedside grinning.

The range of emotions that pounded me was wide enough to reach from one end of a piano to the other; I had feelings to match all eighty-eight keys. Inside my head I could hear every note being thumped out at once.

"Your *first* baby?" the nurse asked.

I nodded, cuddling my daughter. An encompassing emptiness surged within me. "I love her. I'm grateful. I'm scared."

The nurse winked and patted me softly on the shoulder. "I've got eight kids and fourteen grandchildren. You poor, pitiful, mother-of-one, you'll learn. Babies make great teachers. You'll both survive."

It's been nearly two decades, and five more children since my initiating moments of motherhood. Miracle of miracles, we have survived. *Only* because that emptiness within me has been filled by the bounty that Heavenly Father offers to all of us.

Motherhood has turned out to be the paramount joy of my life. The love I feel for my children has intensified and expanded. So has the fear that I'll commit some unpardonable wrong that will harm my children. I still can't keep a houseplant alive. But I have learned that kids are easier to maintain than houseplants; they let you know when they need to be watered, and they maneuver on their own toward sunlight. Love them fiercely and dust 'em off once in awhile—kids manage remarkably well. You know why? Because mothers, contrary to my original fears, are *not* alone in this holy and high calling. No woman called to mother a child is ever alone. Even if she does not have a husband, both she and her child always, always have a Father in

Heaven to turn to for advice and guidance. There are teachers, leaders, neighbors, and friends. Most importantly, the Savior's words, "lo, I am with you alway . . ." (Matt. 28:20) should be every mother's mantra.

Life has taught me that I was right and I was wrong. An earthly mother's power to protect her children is limited, her patience sparse at times, her wisdom non-existent at other times. My ability to love, even with a mother's love, was insufficient. But the glorious glad tidings of the gospel is that through grace, we are given all that we lack. The power of the Lord is only a prayer away. His infinite wisdom can be ours. His patience is steadfast, His love unconditional.

To help supplement our family's income, I have spent the past two decades photographing children and families. I saw this as an opportunity to glean wisdom and advice from those who had already accomplished what I was trying to achieve. I've interviewed hundreds of mothers, grandmothers, and great-grandmothers on methods of motherhood. My mother died when I was entering my teenage years. As an orphan, I felt desperate to learn from every good example that I observed. I kept a careful record of responses, advice on what to do and what not to do.

One of the wisest pieces of advice I received was from a West Virginia great-grandmother. She was soft-spoken and genteel. Her body was frail, but her spirit stalwart. I knelt by the side of her wheelchair so our eyes could meet. "Remember," she said, "children aren't the only ones who need to be fed. When the mother deprives herself of her cravings, I'm talking deep-down-in-the-soul yearnings, the whole family's bound to suffer the hunger."

Was she giving me permission to indulge in decadent desserts? No. She was telling me that if I did not feed my spirit true soul-food, I would become malnourished, subject to spiritual disease; and, consequently, my family would suffer.

What type of manna does a mother's spirit need to remain healthy and strong? Jesus explained, "My Father giveth you the true bread from heaven. . . . I am the bread of life: he that cometh to me shall never hunger; and he that believeth on me shall never thirst" (John 6:32, 35).

The concept once baffled me, but Elder Joseph B. Wirthlin explained it tenderly. I was not unlike the Samaritan woman Jesus spoke to at Jacob's well. Christ and his disciples were traveling by foot from Judea to Galilee. The roads were dusty and dry. The party was no doubt hot and hungry when they passed through the Samaritan city of Sychar to pause at Jacob's well. Imagine the thoughts and feelings Jesus felt there, on that historic piece of ground. He was the Son of God but was subjecting himself to the hunger and thirst of mortality. He was weary. The disciples had gone in search of food while Jesus remained at the well.

While resting there, a Samaritan woman approached and Jesus requested that she draw water to quench his thirst. The woman had to have been startled. "Jews and Samaritans were divided by rancor and did not often speak to one another." She asked, "How is it that thou, being a Jew, askest drink of me, which am a woman of Samaria?" (John 4:9).

Christ "took this opportunity to testify of His divine role as the Redeemer of the world. . . . He patiently, yet thoughtfully answered the woman: 'If thou knewest the gift of God, and who it is that saith to thee, Give me to drink; thou wouldest have asked of him, and he would have given thee living water' (John 4:10)."

The woman was "intrigued but skeptical, . . . seeing that Jesus had no container with which to draw water." What was this man's "living water," anyway? Did it taste better than Jacob's well water? Thinking only of satisfying her physical thirst and of her inconvenience, [she] demanded, 'Sir, give me this water, that I thirst not, neither come hither to draw' (John 4:15)."

Jesus offered a well that will never run dry. "Whosoever drinketh of this water shall thirst again: But whosoever drinketh of the water that I shall give him shall never thirst; but the water that I shall give him shall be in him a well of water springing up into everlasting life"(John 4:13–14).

Jesus offers us the same living water that He offered the Samaritan woman. His pure love. His pure life. An opportunity for our own Eternal life. "Elder Bruce R. McConkie defined living water as 'the words of eternal life, the message of salvation, the truths about God and his kingdom; it is the doctrines of the gospel.' He went on to explain, 'Where there are prophets of God, there will be found rivers of living water, wells filled with eternal truths, springs bubbling forth their life-giving draughts that save from spiritual death.' ("Living Water to Quench Spiritual Thirst," *Ensign*, May 1995, 18).

Keep in mind that this Samaritan woman was not exactly the picture of virtue, yet Jesus did not hesitate to offer her a feast for the soul, an opportunity for a renewal of life—the same invitation He extends to each of us, no matter our infirmities or infractions.

The conversation between Jesus and the Samaritan woman continued. The Savior, seer that He was, knew this woman and knew the details of her life, just like He knows ours. When she realized who He was she went into the city telling what had transpired and asking, "Is not this the Christ?" (John 4:29).

Meanwhile, Christ's disciples returned with a meal. "I have meat to eat that ye know not of," replied the Master (John 4:32).

Confusion rippled through the crowd. Can't you just picture Peter whispering to Andrew, "What's He talking about? Who brought Jesus supper? How did they get here before we did?"

But Jesus was not talking meat and potatoes. He was referring to spiritual food when He said, "My meat is to do the will of him that sent me, and to finish his work" (John 4:34).

Whoa. Talk about manna to a mother's hungry soul. Ever since I was blessed with the responsibility of motherhood, my constant desire has been to rear my children in righteousness, to raise them "up unto the Lord." My manna is to do the will of Him who sent my children into my care. To finish His work.

But how can we know that we are doing the will of Him who entrusts us with children? And how can we ever know when our work is finished? The world would say a mother's work is done when she draws her final breath. Not for Latter-day Saint mothers. Even after death, our responsibilities, coupled with our joys, continue.

We live in a world where women suffer spiritual malnourishment. Elder Jeffrey R. Holland deems it "spiritual anorexia." We are famished for something more than Chinese food, a meal that leaves us hungry ten minutes after we stuff ourselves.

No wonder I felt so famished, so fearful. But I was wrong in thinking that I was alone in my calling. No mother is ever alone, left in the wilderness to fend for herself and her children. Elder Henry B. Eyring's assurance speaks right to a mother's heart. "There will be times when you will feel overwhelmed. One of the ways you will be attacked is with the feeling that you are inadequate. Well, you are inadequate to answer a call to represent God with only your own powers. But you have access to more than your natural capacities, and you do not work alone" (Henry B. Eyring, "Rise to Your Call," *Ensign*, Nov. 2002, 76).

I think back to my childhood and to my own mother. She was widowed with two small children. Her life had been linked together by a string of tragedies, and she attempted to quench her thirst with alcohol. How would our lives have been altered if she had turned to heaven instead? I don't know if she even knew how to pray. I never heard her pray. I never saw her read the scriptures. My heart aches to imagine the emptiness she must have suffered.

Yet, I have something my mother never had. I have a knowledge of the gospel and access to blessings that could have been hers had she known. Dear Sisters, we are supremely blessed to have a knowledge of the gospel of Jesus Christ. We know who we are. We know who our children are. We know that motherhood is not a job, but a calling. We know we are in parental partnership with Heavenly Father, who loves all of His children.

Such knowledge does not protect us from pain nor does it ensure a problem-free life. What it does offer is a guiding light that never dims, a feast that is always set before us, a banquet of bread that does not grow moldy and a well of water that never becomes stale. A knowledge of the gospel gives us a ready supply of spiritual sustenance. It is up to us, as Latter-day Saints, as women of faith, as mothers in Zion, to share our bounty.

Word of the Savior's miraculous feeding of 5,000 people in the Galilee with only five barley loaves and two fishes attracted throngs of hungry followers seeking a free meal. Elder Holland explained, "That food, important as it was, was incidental to the real nourishment He was trying to give them.

'Your fathers did eat manna in the wilderness, and are dead.' He admonished them . . . 'I am the living bread which came down from heaven: if any man eat of this bread, he shall live for ever' (John 6:49, 51)" ("He Hath Filled the Hungry with Good Things," *Ensign*, Nov. 1997, 65).

Like the Samaritan woman, Christ's concept was hard for the Galileans to understand; they were barely anticipating bread and fish, not spiritual manna. What follows, I think, is one of the saddest sentences in all of scripture. "From that time many of his disciples went back, and walked no more with him" (John 6:66).

I can picture that scene.

I can sense the Savior's pain.

I can also understand the disciples' decision.

They were confused. Disappointed. Faithless. Those are states of emotion that I have experienced. Too many times I want the answers to my prayers to be clear, immediate, and satisfying. But that's not the way faith works. We *know* the will of the Lord when we *do* the will of the Lord. "Do my will to know my will," say the scriptures (see John 7:17). I want to know that I'm doing the will of the Father. No woman needs to worry that her work is in vain.

I wish I could give you a simple recipe for manna that is fool-proof. If every hungry mother mixes three hours of prayer with ten hours of service baked during two separate temple visits—voila—her soul is full! I might as well tell you how to molten a mountain. Manna is a miracle only the Lord can provide.

When the Israelites grew hungry they simply had to step outside their tents and pick up what the Lord provided. I believe it is *almost* that easy for us. We have to "pick up" the scriptures, but also do as Nephi admonished, "*feast* upon the words of Christ; for behold, the words of Christ will tell you all things what ye should do"(2 Ne. 32:3, emphasis added). The scriptures are a manual for motherhood.

When we want to know how to be a better parent, the scriptures teach us what kind of parent Heavenly Father is to us. When we seek inspiration for a needy child, the scriptures present us with guidance. They teach us to fast, to serve, to pray. In essence they teach us how to feed ourselves with what the Lord provides. Answers, like manna, can rain down from heaven through pure intelligence flowing into us, giving us "sudden strokes of ideas" (*Teachings of the Prophet Joseph Smith*, 151).

I am not a perfect mother. Not even in the vicinity. I fall far short of my aspirations. I say things I wish I hadn't said and I fail to do things I wish I had done. As a mother in Zion I am commanded to "bring up [my] children in light and truth . . ." (D&C 93:40).

I try, but how do I know if I am succeeding?

Nephi reminds us that "the Lord giveth no commandments unto the children of men, save he shall prepare a way for them that they may accomplish the thing which he commandeth them" (1 Ne. 3:7).

The scriptures are my guide. When I think motherhood is painful, I am reminded that Eve had no epidurals. No baby books to consult. No pediatricians to prescribe a diaper-rash ointment. No nurse there to teach her how to breastfeed. Our being alive is a testament to Eve's mothering abilities as "the mother of all living." She performed the tasks she was programmed to perform. Picture the joy as Father Adam and Mother Eve cuddle the firstborn baby on planet Earth. I see them overwhelmed and overjoyed with the weight and wonder of the "greatest responsibility God gives to human beings." And I see that baby wrapped in designer leopard-skin diapers—made from real leopards. Imagine changing those beasts!

Fast forward to another scene, one that is not detailed in scriptures, but one that surely transpired. Mother Eve and Father Adam cradling the lifeless body of their son Abel. And how did they deal with the anguish of their son Cain's transgression?

To love is to know pain. And no one knows love or pain like a parent.

As mothers, we have to trust our God-given instincts. We have to trust God. "Lean not to thine own understanding" (Prov. 3:5). Mothers, we are not left to ourselves. We have been programmed by divine design to succeed. To love. To nurture. To *mother*. Father called us. He will provide, support, even magnify us as long as we give motherhood our highest priority, our truest heart.

No matter what your soul craves, what your spirit yearns for, the Master has set the table. An invitation from the Lord of Hosts awaits you; your name is engraved on the envelope. "Come . . . every one that thirsteth, come ye to the waters; and he that hath no money, come buy and eat; yea, come buy wine and milk without money and without price" (2 Ne. 9:50).

After the Samaritan woman went out to tell of her encounter with Christ, a crowd gathered and for two days Jesus tarried to teach and to testify. Echoing those Samaritans who listened to the Savior at Jacob's well, we too can say with faith and with firm conviction, "We have heard him ourselves, and know that this is indeed the Christ, the Saviour of the world" (John 4:42).

It is that sure testimony that assures us that He will feed our voracious spiritual appetites. Sisters, no matter who you mother or how you mother, motherhood is a divine calling that requires us to fortify our spirits with the vitamins and minerals of the gospel. Come, let us dine together; there is manna enough for all. When we arrive and sit down to feast together, let us remain for the entire adventure. Let us not be confused or caught up with our physical fears or desires. Let us feed our spirits, nourish our souls, and never walk away from the finest the Lord has to offer. Let us be the disciples who remain to dine with the Master.

Mary, the mother of Christ, bore testimony that "He hath filled the hungry with good things . . . " (Luke 1:53). He has filled my hungry soul. I promise you that He will do the same for all of us.

CHAPTER TWO

Spiritual Amnesia

Have ye received
his image in your countenances?

—*Alma 5:14*

One day my daughter came home from elementary school with a little booklet she had made as a gift for me. It was entitled "All About My Mother." On the cover was a stick figure of a woman who was supposed to be me. I like stick figures—they make me look thin. The woman had big red lips curved into an eager smile, and she was holding the hand of a towheaded child dressed in pink—my daughter, I surmised.

Inside there was a questionnaire filled out in bright blue crayon. *My mother's name is . . . My mother's favorite food is . . . My mother was born in . . .* For a second grader, I was impressed with the accuracy of her answers. My daughter knew more about me than I realized. And then came the question: *My mother's hair color is . . .* and my daughter wrote with excruciating honesty . . . "she's changed it so much no one can remember."

I hadn't thought about that story until the other day when a girlfriend of mine asked that I offer a prayer in her behalf. She desired a specific blessing.

"Sure," I agreed, "I'll pray for you, as long as you pray for yourself."

A look of pain and confusion crossed her face. "I haven't prayed in twenty years."

I was shocked. My friend was a good woman with a generous heart. Though she was now inactive, she had grown up in a home where the gospel was taught and lived. "Why haven't you prayed?" I asked.

"God wouldn't listen to me if I did."

"How do you know?"

"Because I've committed too many sins." She went on to list a barrage of broken commandments.

Isn't it funny how we humans foolishly think we can dictate our Heavenly Father's behavior? Because we act a certain way, we anticipate how God will react. But our Father in Heaven does not react. Our behavior does not alter His. "There is a God in heaven, who is infinite and eternal, from everlasting to everlasting the same unchangeable God, the framer of heaven and earth, and all things which are in them" (D&C 20:17). "For I know that God is not a partial God, neither a changeable being; but he is unchangeable from all eternity to all eternity" (Moro. 8:18).

I listened as my friend described a divine being whom I did not know, a god who was petty, temperamental, and unforgiving. "I don't recognize this Deity you describe," I said.

"The truth is, I've changed so much I don't remember God," my friend replied. Then she paused before reflecting, "There are times I don't even remember who I am."

I prayed for my friend. I continue to pray for her. I pray for myself, because there are times when sin, like cataracts, clouds my spiritual vision.

Sisters, who are we—really? How can we know our Father in Heaven and our place as His daughters?

The Savior taught, "This is life eternal, that they might know thee the only true God, and Jesus Christ, whom thou hast sent" (John 17:3).

Painful as it was, my friend's disobedience had kept her from remembering who she was, who God is. The Apostle John taught, "And hereby we do know that we know him, if we keep his commandments. He that saith, I know him, and keepeth not his commandments, is a liar, and the truth is not in him. But whoso keepeth his word, in him verily is the love of God perfected: hereby know we that we are in him. He that saith he abideth in him ought himself also so to walk, even as he walked" (1 Jn. 2:3–6).

We can know our Father by emulating our Father. The only way to emulate Him is to study and know the paths He walked and to follow in those footsteps.

As we come to know our Father, our own spiritual identity is revealed. Divine Ancestry 101 can begin any number of ways, but will always require an in-depth, spirit-guided tutorial of God's nature. The Bible Dictionary defines God as "The supreme Governor of the universe and the Father of mankind. We learn from the revelations that have been given that there are three separate persons in the Godhead: the Father, the Son, and the Holy Ghost. . . . When one speaks of God, it is generally the Father who is referred to; that is, Elohim. All mankind are his children. . . . [M]ankind has a special relationship to him that differentiates man from all other created things: man is literally God's offspring, made in his image" (Bible Dictionary, 681–82).

No more savory manna could be set before us than such knowledge, but knowing *about* God is very different from knowing God. That knowledge comes only through the Spirit and cannot be withheld from anyone who sincerely seeks to *know* Him. "The Lord has indicated that the gates of hell cannot prevail against revelation from him to any one of his children who desires to know the living God and to know the living Jesus Christ. This is available by divine commitment and by divine will, that for anyone desiring to know God the Eternal Father and to know his Son Jesus Christ, God is under commitment and the gates of hell cannot prevail against that commitment; and it will be revealed through the power and principle of revelation direct from God to the one desiring to receive that information" (Bernard P. Brockbank, "Knowing God," *Ensign*, July 1972, 121).

I testify to you that as we come to know God, our Father, we will come to know ourselves. When is the last time you looked into a mirror and saw a daughter of God looking back at you?

Even with all of our flaws and frailties, we are the children of Deity, entitled to an eternal inheritance if we but keep our Father's mandates. Maybe you've heard this truth all of your life. Maybe the revelation is new to you. As Latter-day Saints we sing about our divine ancestry each time we sing the Primary song, "I Am a Child of God."

We hear it.

We sing it.

We preach it.

But do we truly believe it? Do we really *know* that a loving Father in Heaven, the all-powerful Elohim, is the Father of our spirits? Do we know that He loves us? That we have access to him through our

Redeemer and Elder Brother, Jesus Christ? Do we know that as insignificant as we may feel at times, we are never insignificant to Heavenly Father?

For decades I struggled with self-esteem issues. I felt unworthy, unlovable, incapable, and inferior. At the very moment when I should have felt most confident, when I became a mother, I felt lower than a dust bunny. Therapists tell me it's because I was abused as a child. I believe it's because Satan strikes hardest when we are most vulnerable. His diabolical mind knows that if he can wound the mother, he can weaken the child. Peter's warning seems especially applicable to mothers of the latter days. "Be sober, be vigilant; because your adversary the devil as a roaring lion, walketh about, seeking whom he may devour" (1 Pet. 5:8).

Satan wants to devour us. One very effective and destructive way he does that is to cloud our spiritual vision with self-debasing thoughts. He convinces us to sin, and the minute that we do, he then condemns us for the very act he connived us into committing. The devil misled me into thinking that all of my self-debasing remarks were founded in humility. I wasn't being humble. I was being harmful. Every time I put myself down, I had two small daughters who heard me. One day when they were well on their way to womanhood, I listened carefully to what they were saying about themselves. It broke my heart to hear my girls pass self-judgments, the same judgments they had heard me pronounce on myself so many times. "I'm fat. I'm stupid. I'm ugly. I have no talent. I am not worthy."

"But you're wrong," I said. "You are beautiful, you are intelligent, you are blessed. You *are* worthy. Why can't you see that?" I marched my eldest daughter to the bathroom mirror and said, "Take a hard look and tell me who you see."

She stood there for a long time. I expected her to announce, "I see a daughter of God." Instead, she said, "I see *you*, Mom. When I look at me, I see *you*."

Ouch!

The truths we learn from our children. My soul hungered for help. I turned to the scriptures and discovered what I should have known all along. The Savior never once put Himself down. The same veil that shadows our memories of the premortal existence shielded His mortal eyes. Only as He "went about doing good" (Acts 10:38), and "the will of the Father" (John 5:30), was His true identity and purpose revealed to Him. Jesus Christ never wasted His thoughts, His words, or His actions on being negative or feeling sorry for Himself.

The prophets, human as they are, never say, "I can't stand in front of all those people to preach; I'm too fat." Okay, so Jonah hesitated, tried to run, and we all know how that turned out.

The Lord is mindful of our strengths and our weaknesses. He knew that Moses suffered a speech impediment, so He provided a mouthpiece in Aaron. He knew that Nephi suffered from feelings of unworthiness, that Elijah was prone to bouts of depression. Still, because they discovered who they "were in Christ," those prophets were able to fulfill their missions with faith and fortitude.

When I converted to the Church, Spencer W. Kimball was the prophet. He was extraordinarily loved and revered. But Spencer W. Kimball, by the world's standards, was not prophet material. He was an insurance salesman. He stood only a few inches taller than I do. And he suffered a plethora of health problems. Following one of his throat surgeries, Spencer Kimball was left with no voice at all. "During a testimony meeting in the temple, President David O. McKay asked him to bear his testimony. He could not speak a word. He could only utter inaudible, breathy sounds. He wrote a note to President McKay afterwards and asked, 'Why would you do that to me?' President McKay's reply was one of a true prophet, filled with love and seership. 'Spencer, you must get your voice back, for you still have a great mission to perform'" (Robert D. Hales, "Examples from the Life of a Prophet," *Ensign*, Nov. 1981, 19).

I might have been humiliated and hurt. Not Spencer W. Kimball. Instead of humiliation, he chose humility. He remained steadfast in his obedience. "He learned how to control the air in his throat and to use scar tissue that developed in his larynx and his remaining vocal cord. And he manipulated that until he regained a voice that bore a mighty testimony to the world—as a prophet of God.

Spencer W. Kimball knew who he was in Christ. The world would have us believe the greatest confidence we can achieve is self-confidence; but the only real confidence is an abiding faith in Jesus Christ, the One who knows us, loves us, and stands ready to span the distance between where we are and where we need to be.

Through a sincere spiritual search I slowly gained confidence, not in myself, but in my Savior, and who I am in Him. I didn't gain that divine understanding from a self-help seminar or a best-selling book; my therapist was the Holy Ghost. Line upon line, experience upon experience, through personal revelation, I began to see myself as a child of God. What surprised me most was that the revelation did not seem new; it struck me as a reminder. I was slowly recovering from "spiritual amnesia."

Do you remember who you are, who you were prior to this life? Do you know who you can become?

WHO WE WERE THEN

Life is eternal. We existed before our earthly birthdates. "Preexistence is not some remote and mysterious place," taught Elder Bruce R. McConkie. "All of us are but a few years removed from the Eternal Presence, from him whose children we are and in whose house we dwelt. All of us are separated by a thin veil only from the friends and fellow laborers with whom we served on the Lord's errand before our eternal spirits took up their abodes in tabernacles of clay.

"True, a curtain has been drawn so we do not recall our associations there. But we do know that our Eternal Father has all power, all might, all dominion, and all truth and that he lives in the family unit. We do know that we are his children, created in his image, endowed with power and ability to become like him. We know he gave us our agency and ordained the laws by obedience to which we can obtain eternal life. We know we had friends and associates there. We know we were schooled and trained and taught in the most perfect educational system ever devised, and that by obedience to his eternal laws we developed infinite varieties and degrees of talents.

"And hence comes the doctrine of foreordination. When we come into mortality, we bring the talents, capacities, and abilities acquired by obedience to law in our prior existence. Mozart composed and published sonatas when but eight years of age because he was born with musical talent. Melchizedek came into this world with such faith and spiritual capacity that 'when a child he feared God, and stopped the mouths of lions, and quenched the violence of fire' (JST, Gen. 14:26)," ("God Foreordained His Prophets and His People," *Ensign*, May 1974, 73).

What skills did we bring into mortality? What skills can we develop? Which relationships can we renew and establish while on earth? How about the one with ourselves? Had my friend really changed so much that she was unrecognizable, even to herself? If so, it is a state that does not have to be permanent. Repentance, I have learned, is like cataract surgery; the veil lifts and, once again, we can see clearly.

May the Spirit enlighten our minds and hearts to remember and to realize that within us is divine seed. When life grows dark and our spirits hunger, may we turn to the scriptures and feast on the plain truths found in the Plan of Salvation. When the world whispers that we don't belong, that we don't matter, may we pray and ponder. Let us forgo physical food as we fast to stretch our faith, to strengthen our spiritual muscles until we can lift that veil of spiritual amnesia.

Who We Are Now

If we could see with unveiled eyes, we would know that life, in spite of the pain and the problems, has divine purpose. We would have no doubt that we are known and loved as individuals, that our stations in life were not achieved by a roll of the dice.

We are daughters reserved to be born in these latter days for a reason. On the matter of being born into the House of Israel, President Harold B. Lee said, "Surely [this] must have been determined by the kind of lives we had lived in that premortal spirit world. Some may question these assumptions, but at the same time they will accept without any question the belief that each one of us will be judged when we leave this earth according to his or her deeds during our lives here in mortality. Isn't it just as reasonable to believe that what we have received here in this earth life was given to each of us according to the merits of our conduct before we came here?" (Understanding Who We Are Brings Self-Respect," *Ensign*, January 1974, 5).

We are also mothers in Zion and the magnitude of that calling should never be demeaned or underestimated. Elder Matthew Cowley taught that "men have to have something given to them [in mortality] to make them saviors of men, but not mothers, not women. [They] are born with an inherent right, an inherent authority, to be the saviors of human souls . . . and the regenerating force in the lives of God's children" (*Matthew Cowley Speaks*, 109).

It is an absolute and terrifying truth that Satan is out to "devour us." His sole design is destruction. He wants my friend to believe that because she has sinned, she cannot pray. He wants us all to feel unworthy, unclean, and unlovable. But nowhere in scripture does the Lord turn away those who seek Him. His promise is peace in the midst of chaos. He has given us His word, His love, His strength. I testify to you that the Lord's strength is greater than the adversary's. His wisdom will not fail us when we are confronted with evil. The battle will always go to the believers, for they battle with a might that cannot be matched. His promise is sure. "I will not suffer that they [the enemy] shall destroy my work; yea, I will show unto them that my wisdom is greater than the cunning of the devil" (D&C 10:43).

We must trust. We must trust the Lord's love, the Lord's strength, the Lord's wisdom—never more than when our own fails us.

WHO WE CAN BECOME

The concept of "becoming" is dear to my heart. For so long I felt stuck in the mire of life. Only the gospel of Jesus Christ pulled me out and allowed me to get up and get about my Father's business, to forget myself and remember Him whose errand I was on.

As Latter-day Saint women, we should all be Mothers in Israel. Whether or not we have given birth to children, we can love, nurture, guide, and protect God's little ones. It is our right and our responsibility to raise the rising generation. President Gordon B. Hinckley spoke directly to us, the women of the Church, when he challenged: "Rise to the great potential within you. I do not ask that you reach beyond your capacity. I hope you will not nag yourselves with thoughts of failure. I hope you will not try to set goals far beyond your capacity to achieve. I hope you will simply do what you can do in the best way you know. If you do so, you will witness miracles come to pass" (*Motherhood: A Heritage of Faith,* 1995, 9).

Read that quote again. President Hinckley says, "I hope you will not nag yourselves with thoughts of failure."

He is a prophet, a man who knows a woman's heart. Too often we forget who we were, who we are, who we can become. We set ourselves up for failure by not defining ourselves as who we are, but rather by *what* we are not. I used to define myself as the woman who was not skinny enough, pretty enough, smart enough. I couldn't bake rolls that were flaky enough, or make a garden grow that weeds didn't choke. With every negative definition, I blinded myself to the vision of my true identity. I wasn't this and I wasn't that. All of those *wasn'ts* got in the way of who I was—who I *am*—who I can become.

We are daughters of God, and "so [our] needs are great" (*Hymns*, 301). Perhaps our greatest need is to know that we are loved. Love is the most powerful force on earth. God so loved the world that He gave His beloved Son. Never allow the adversary to convince you that because you are not perfect, you are not lovable. The Apostle Paul taught, "God commendeth his love toward us, in that, while we were yet sinners, Christ died for us" (Rom. 5:8).

How would our lives change if, when we looked into the mirror, we saw a spark of divinity shining forth? If we could really see our spiritual parentage in our mortal selves?

Many sisters look "good" on the outside—many who come to church and sit next to us in Relief Society. They appear to have it all together, but what inward wounds do those outward appearances hide? My friend's disobedience had injured her so severely that she felt unworthy to pray. "I only attend church when there is a special occasion," she confessed, "and I make sure I look good. I don't want anyone to suspect how I really feel."

"The Lord looketh on the heart" (1 Sam. 16:7). He sees beyond appearances. He loves us in spite of our faults and failings. He has provided the way, the only way, for us to heal, to become whole and clean—to recognize and see ourselves as He sees us. "Only the life, teachings, and particularly the Atonement of Jesus Christ can release us from this otherwise impossible predicament. Each of us has made mistakes, large or small, which if unresolved will keep us from the presence of God. For this reason, the Atonement of Jesus Christ is the single most significant event that ever has or ever will occur. This selfless act of infinite consequence, performed by a single glorified personage, has eternal impact in the life of every son and daughter of our Father in Heaven—without exception" (Richard G. Scott, "Finding Forgiveness," *Ensign*, May 1995, 75).

Jesus Christ never forgot who He was. He was ever mindful of His Father. Yet that knowledge did not dismiss Him from the suffering and trials of mortality. We humans, we mothers of the flesh, must remember, we do not work alone.

We have an extended and eternal family, separated by a very thin veil, working with us as we strive to do our Father's will. If we have altered ourselves through sin, so that we do not recognize the woman in the mirror or the Father who waits patiently for our call, may we make the changes necessary to restore our true identity. May we all put our lives in order so that we can know God the Father and His Son. May we be worthy to be led and lifted by the Holy Spirit. May we look into the mirror, and see the woman that Father sees, an eternal being who is reflected back at us—not an image defined by the world, but a daughter of Deity with an identity familiar on both sides of the veil. Our destiny is to remember who we were, recall who we are, and realize who we can become.

CHAPTER THREE

Lessons Learned from a Messy House

She looketh well to the ways of her household,
and eateth not the bread of idleness.
——*Proverbs 31:27*

A husband came home from work one evening to find total mayhem in his house. His children were outside, still in their pajamas, wrestling in the mud, with empty food boxes and wrappers strewn all around the front yard. The door of his wife's car was open, as was the front door to the house. Inside, he found an even larger mess. A lamp had been knocked over, and the throw rug was wadded against one wall. In the family room the dog who always stayed outside was curled up on the sofa watching cartoons. The front room (the *home teaching room,* which was always spotless) was littered with toys and various items of clothing. In the kitchen, dishes filled the sink, breakfast food was spilled on the counter, dog food was spilled on the floor, a broken glass lay under the table, and a small pile of sand was spread by the back door. He quickly headed up the stairs, stepping over toys and more piles of clothes, looking for his wife. He was worried she may be ill, or that something serious had happened. He found her lounging in the bedroom, still curled in the bed in her pajamas, reading a novel. She looked up at him, smiled, and asked how his day went. He looked at her, bewildered, and asked, "What happened here today?"

She again smiled and answered, "You know every day when you come home from work and ask me what in the world I did today?"

"Yes," was his incredulous reply.

She answered, "Well, today I didn't do it."

I love this story. I love it because it makes me feel like maybe, just maybe, all my homemaking efforts are not in vain. And maybe if I stayed in bed or took a vacation to Madagascar, someone would notice by the end of the day.

One of Satan's ways of discouraging us is to convince us that the work we do, day in and day out, does not matter. It matters. C. S. Lewis wrote, "A housewife's work . . . is the one for which all others exist" (*The Quotable Lewis,* 191).

I believe that there is a difference between housekeeping and homemaking. Society has demeaned the term "housewife" until it is shameful. There is nothing shameful in the task when it is done with care and love. In a revelation to the Prophet Joseph Smith, the Lord commands us, "Organize yourselves; prepare every needful thing; and establish a house, even a house of prayer, a house of fasting, a house of faith, a house of learning, a house of glory, a house of order, a house of God" (D&C 88:119). President Ezra Taft Benson stated, "One great thing the Lord requires of each of us is to provide a home where a happy, positive influence for good exists" ("Great Things Required of Their Fathers,"*Ensign*, May 1981, 34).

I contend that there is a dimension of difference between a house and a home. We see photographs of houses in magazines where everything appears "picture perfect." Color coordinated. Everything is brand spanking new. I've lived in houses like that. They are not homes.

Homes are supposed to be heaven on earth and we, as the mothers, are supposed to be the heart of those homes. President Spencer W. Kimball wrote: "Heaven is a place, but also a condition; it is home and family. It is understanding and kindness. . . . It is quiet, sane living; personal sacrifice, genuine hospitality, wholesome concern for others. It is living the commandments of God" (*Faith Precedes the Miracle*, 265).

A house can be built of mortar and brick, mud and thatch. It takes love and the Lord to make that edifice a home. "Except the Lord build the house, they labour in vain that build it" (Ps. 127:1).

A day does not go by when I don't wish I were a better housekeeper. It is not one of my inherent skills. I have neighbors who, when their houses are spotless, go outside to sift the soil in their flowerbeds. I sometimes forget to drain the spaghetti. Should I stone myself because I fall short of what I know I should be doing?

Absolutely not.

But I do.

I keep thinking one of these days we'll be able to hire help. Our house will be a house of order, a place of peace, and I can take all the credit for the work the maid does. We've been married over twenty years, and there is still no maid in sight. In the meantime, the Lord has shown me a way to improve my housekeeping and homemaking skills that I would like to share with you.

My father's mother was a housekeeper. She was the mother of all housekeepers. Sarah Lillian Sorenson never quite weighed a hundred pounds (except for when she was pregnant). She never stood five feet tall, even on her tippy-toes. She never learned to drive a car or boot up a computer. But Grandma could shoe a horse, milk a cow, kill and dress a chicken, and shoot a rifle straight and deadly.

She could hitch a wagon and walk faster than most of her children could run. Once when a rabid dog threatened her family, she faced it down with only a dirt clod for a weapon. She carded wool to make quilts, boiled lye to make soap, and tatted lace to make her humble home more beautiful.

Her parents immigrated to Sanpete County, Utah, from Copenhagen, Denmark, and so Grandma was bilingual, though she never graduated from high school. She married my grandfather, a farmer who stood well over six feet tall. Together, they raised eight children, all of whom towered over Grandma by the time they were twelve years old.

"God made me to be a mother," she often said. Her family was her life and her life was hard. Grandma called the Sanpete soil "talcum dry" and the ever-blowing wind "her constant companion."

In spite of those conditions, Grandma was renowned for her housekeeping skills (none of which I inherited); dust fled in fear when Grandma got out her rag and bees' wax furniture polish.

To give you a true picture of my grandmother's housekeeping skills, here's a stanza from a family poem presented when Grandma's ward Relief Society honored her.

There's our Lillian, the beautiful,
Just as good as she is dutiful.
She mops and scrubs from seven to seven
For Lil could find cobwebs in the Kingdom of heaven!

I share Grandma's sentiment: God made me to be a mother. But Grandma and I mother our children very differently, not only because we live in different eras, but because we are individual women. Our children are equally unique. Should I feel guilty that I think of dust, not as something to be eradicated, but more like a protective covering? (It sort of makes the house all warm and fuzzy. Okay, only fuzzy.) I absolutely should *not* feel guilty. There's no room for guilt in the gospel; remorse yes, as long as it prompts us to repent and move onward and upward. But guilt? No way. No how. Why? Because an immaculate house can't teach our children nearly as much as a messy house. Do not misunderstand me. The Lord's house, the house we are to pattern our homes after, " is a house of order . . ." (D&C 132:8). It is also a house of learning, and some lessons can't be learned without making a mess (making chocolate chip cookies with a two year old, for example).

I am not advocating uncleanliness—"no unclean thing can dwell [in the Kingdom of Heaven]" (Moses 6:57). But there is a significant difference between uncleanliness and messiness. I know whereof I write. I live in a house where children run and play and eat and sleep. Where they bathe frogs in the bathtub and sneak the dog in at night to sleep beneath the bed. Just this summer we rescued a wounded hawk, and its favored perch was the arm of our new sofa. Such adventures are the reason we've been blessed with antibacterial soap and rubber gloves.

I've lived in dozens of foster homes. I've been mothered by dozens of women. I've learned something from all of them, mainly that there's a lesson in just about every experience life offers.

President David O. McKay recognized the tremendous responsibility parents have to teach children the gospel. "The first and most important inner quality you can instill in a child is faith in God. The first and most important action a child can learn is obedience. And the most powerful tool you have with which to teach a child is love" (*Instructor*, Vol. 84, Dec. 1949, 620).

What better opportunity to bond with your children than while cleaning the house? You scoff! Perhaps because you know my children. They whine when it comes to housecleaning. They hide. They come down with invisible "chicken pops." My son Dallas swears he's afraid of the broom. I understand his fear; the vacuum terrifies me.

Not one of my children takes after their great-grandmother Sorenson.

"Why can't you be more like her?" I asked my daughter.

She squinted at a dusty photograph and said, "She's *dead,* Mom."

"Right. But still . . ."

"Isn't Great-Grandma Sorenson the one who ironed her garments and rewashed the dishes after you did them for her?"

I nodded.

"Why can't *you* be more like her, Mom?"

"Come on," I said, "let's go for a bike ride."

It doesn't always work. Some kids love to clean, others don't. Some mothers love to clean. Others don't. Regardless, a clean house is a blessing to everyone who resides there. What I am advocating is that we mothers get rid of the guilt and start taking advantage of an opportunity we may be wasting—working side-by-side with our children.

You cringe because it is so much easier for a mother to pitch in and do the work than it is to be slowed down by a whining, whimpering child, or a child who is so gung-ho to clean that he empties an entire spray bottle of bleach on the new livingroom drapes.

Patience, it is said, is developed ONLY under trial.

So imagine your house. Now imagine it messy. Not dirty, just messy. It's got that lived-in look in every room. Now imagine you're poised to polish, and at your heels is a child or two. Your approach will depend on the age of your children. It won't matter, as long as you work *together.*

First, you go to a room and play "Count Your Blessings." That means you pick up the items that are out of place and put them where they go. You pick up a pair of shoes and talk about how blessed you are to own shoes. "Do you know there are children who don't have shoes?" you ask.

"Name them," your oldest child challenges.

Don't let this throw you. "Debbie, Marie, Amad, Gwen, Mike . . ." you say. Mostly though, you listen. I think mothers should ask twice as many questions as they answer.

Picking up blessings instead of clothes or shoes or toys is a game of gratitude; it turns a chore into an adventure.

When Grandma raised her family, shoes were so scarce that children were lucky if they owned two pairs—one for work and one for dress. Since children in those days walked pretty much everywhere they went, shoes wore out a lot faster than Nikes do today. That presented no real problem during the summers, when kids ran barefoot. Come winter, Grandma would wrap newspaper around her children's feet to plug the holes in the soles to fight against frostbite.

Recognizing a pair of shoes as a blessing opens up endless opportunities to teach and learn the law of gratitude. To learn that gratitude not expressed does no one any good. To learn that when we are grateful for the small things, we can expect even more blessings. "And he who receiveth all things with thankfulness shall be made glorious; and the things of this earth shall be added unto him, even an hundred fold, yea, more" (D&C 78:19).

Count your blessings one at a time, but do it together.

As you scrub the kitchen table and chairs, turn the chairs around so they face outward. Why? Because that's what Grandma did every morning. Unlike me, she believed that there was such a thing as woman's work and such a thing as man's work (though she did both when needed). I don't differentiate; for me, work is just work. But I didn't live in a time and in a place where the family rose before the sun, the men went outside to milk cows and do chores, and the women stayed inside to prepare breakfast. When chores were done and breakfast was ready, the men came in, washed up, and joined the women to kneel, each member at a kitchen chair turned outward. Then family prayer was offered, thanking the Lord for the day, for the breakfast, invoking heaven's blessings to continue with each family member.

Only then were grateful, hungry family members allowed to turn their chairs back toward the table to begin their meal.

Is prayer worth all of that effort? Ask your child. Ask for suggestions on how you can improve your own family prayers. Teaching moments are very different than preaching moments. We can preach anytime, but the Spirit has to be present if teaching is to take place. There are few lessons in life more important than the power of prayer. President Kimball stated: "The Lord has not promised us freedom from adversity or affliction. Instead, he has given us the avenue of communication known as prayer, whereby we might humble ourselves and seek his help and divine guidance, so that we could establish a house of prayer" ("Fortify Your Homes Against Evil," *Ensign*, May 1979, 6).

While you're already down there on your knees with the chairs facing outward, why not pray together?

Sweep out the corners. Clean beneath the sofa cushions. If you are really feeling courageous, scour behind the refrigerator. You're bound to find a lost coin, which provides an opportunity for dual lessons. One in tithing, the other in how important each and every person is in the Lord's heart.

Grandma raised her children during the Great Depression. Money was truly as precious as gold. During the summer months, the older children worked in the fields topping sugar beets. At the end of the day they were fortunate to bring home a quarter, or up to fifty cents if their employer was feeling extremely generous. A fistful of change for eight hours of hard labor! The adults didn't fare a whole lot better; a dollar a day for wages was not uncommon. Grandma's children would come home tired and hungry and she would greet them with a smile and a home-cooked meal. She provided each child with a special container for tithing. Each child would drop in a few pennies, a nickel, a dime, ten percent of their day's earnings. Grandma wore an apron and, from the front pocket, could make proper change if needed.

"Pay the Lord first," she said, "and I promise you that you will never want for the necessities in life."

Every one of her children tested that promise and found it to hold true.

The lost coin also provides an opportunity to teach your children of your love for the scriptures, to teach them of the Savior's love for each child. Kids adore stories almost as much as mothers do. One of my favorites is the parable of the lost coin. I'm always losing things: my money, my keys, my memory.

The woman in the parable is as careless as I can sometimes be. She has ten pieces of silver and drops one. It rolls away from her and is lost. Instead of moaning or feeling sorry for herself, she gets the broom out and starts sweeping in previously unswept corners. She even lights a candle and searches diligently until the coin is found.

What does she do then? She celebrates! "She calleth her friends and her neighbours together, saying, Rejoice with me; for I have found the piece which I had lost" (Luke 15:9). Then comes the lesson that must not be missed. Even when, through our own carelessness, we are lost, the Lord wants us found. We matter to Him! "Likewise, I say unto you, there is joy in the presence of the angels of God over one . . . that repenteth" (Luke 5:10).

Some of my most joyous moments come in hearing my children teach the gospel to me. I tell them a story from the scriptures and the following Monday night they retell the story for family home evening. If they are old enough, they read, then "liken all scriptures unto us" (1 Ne. 19:23). Children's interpretations are always more insightful than mine, and their tellings always more delightful.

Once my son told me that faith is like milk.

"Milk—how so?"

"If you don't take care of it, it gets rotten."

There were no grocery stores when and where Grandma lived. No manna fell from heaven. If they wanted a gallon of milk, they took a bucket and went to visit Old Bossy, the cow. If they wanted to keep the milk cool, they had to cut ice from a frozen lake, pack the ice in sawdust and keep it in a special shed during the summer months. Then they had to saw chunks of that ice to maintain their "icebox." If they wanted bread, they hitched the wagon and took a load of homegrown grain to the mill to have it ground into flour. If they wanted chicken for Sunday dinner . . . Let's just say they didn't go to KFC.

Living by their hard work and God's bounty, Grandma managed to put three hearty meals on the table each and every day, but it was the spiritual manna that she fed her children that nourished them most: how to work, how to serve, how to pray.

Teaching our children the gospel is serious business. The Lord didn't beat around the bush when he declared, "Inasmuch as parents have children in Zion, or in any of her stakes which are organized, that teach them not to understand the doctrine of repentance, faith in Christ the Son of the living God, and of baptism and the gift of the Holy Ghost by the laying on of the hands, when eight years old, the sin be upon the heads of the parents" (D&C 68: 25).

Elder Jacob de Jager tells a story that illustrates how important it is to teach correct principles. I've always related his example to teaching our children. He was at a Regional Representative seminar in 1972.

> At the end of that seminar President Marion G. Romney, on his way out of the auditorium, walked through the aisle where I was standing with two big binders under one arm and a stack of printed materials under the other arm. President Romney stopped and said, "Now, Brother de Jager, how are you going to teach all these inspired materials?"
>
> I paused, thinking of an answer that would satisfy a member of the First Presidency of the Church. I replied, "President Romney, I shall teach in such a way that everyone will understand."
>
> President Romney, a twinkle in his eye, said, "That's not enough; you shall teach in such a way that no one will misunderstand these divine materials." Then he walked on ("Let There Be No Misunderstanding," *Ensign,* Nov. 1978, 67).

I have learned the best way to instruct a child in the gospel is to present the materials and let the Spirit do the teaching.

Now you are moving through the house with speed, organizing, straightening, cleaning. You find yourself in the kitchen, rummaging through cupboards when your child says to you, "Whose dish is this, Mom? It doesn't look familiar."

You look at it and don't recognize it either. It's a glass casserole dish, big and heavy, with an ornate design. It's empty and sparkling so there's no telling what food it once held. You sit at the table with your child and play a game called "Please pass the casserole."

"I think it came from Sister Cherry," you say. "She baked an apple crisp and sent it to us."

"Please pass the casserole," your child says and the dish slides across the table. "I think it belongs to Sister Ward. When you were sick, Mom, she made our family roast beef."

"Please pass the casserole," you say and the dish slides back to you. "It might have come from Brother Clark. He brought us some cucumbers from his garden, remember?"

"I remember."

And you do. As the game progresses, you remember a million kindnesses that have come your way from neighbors, family, friends. Then a wave of guilt hits you. Some wonderful person brought you and your family a generous offering in this dish, and you didn't even have the good manners to return it. What do you do?

"Who is in need of our friendship today?" you ask.

"How about Sister Burr? Her husband just died."

"Great idea." So together you and your child slice fresh peaches and make the best cobbler you can. Actually, you're an experienced mother now, so you make *two*: one for Sister Burr and one for your own family. While the cobbler is still warm you wrap it in a towel and put it in a wagon, then with children in tow, you make a trek through the neighborhood to Sister Burr's house.

She's delighted to see you. When you hand her the cobbler she smiles and says, "Will you look at that, a beautiful dessert, and in the dish I've been searching for all these months! Thank you for returning it."

That's how love works—it moves in a circle that always comes back to you. Charity is love perfected and though we can preach it, there is no better way to teach it than in practice. Charity begins at home.

A burned-out lightbulb is an object lesson in spirituality. Remain in an unlit room together and talk about darkness, how it blackens our vision and we can't see the things that are around us, even though they do not really disappear. Tell the Joseph Smith story, how darkness and fear always come just before the light. Then change the bulb and talk about light. The light of Christ. The light of truth. The light powered by faith and led by the Spirit. If you have a dimmer switch, talk about how we can brighten our lights and keep them shining so that others may see and glorify our Father which is in heaven. Talk all night. Talk until the sun comes up . . . until the *Son* comes up.

I lived in a foster home where the mother refused to purchase a dishwasher until all of her children were grown and moved away, because she cherished the time she spent with them as they tackled a sink full of dirty dishes together. It was her time to quiz them about school, dating, friends. It was their time to pour out their hearts, knowing their hopes and dreams and fears and failures would be safe there at the kitchen sink.

Look around you. Your home is brimming with opportunities to share the gospel with your children, to have them share it with you. Once my son brought me a rotten potato. "You know what this reminds me of?" he asked.

I didn't dare to even venture a guess.

"Leprosy," he said. "See how it's all bumpy and icky-black?"

"I see." I could also smell it.

"One day Jesus was walking through a village and he saw ten guys who looked just like this potato. They had leprosy and so it was against the law for them to be around people who didn't. Jesus fixed them, good as new. Do you know what happened, Mom?"

I knew but waited for his answer.

"Only one of those guys came back to say 'thanks.'"

Oh, Father, how thankful I am for a rotten potato!

Someone once told me that life is one mess after another; if we can just endure to the end, our reward will be a self-cleaning house. Don't we wish!

What I have learned as a mother is that it doesn't really matter who makes the mess; it just has to be cleaned up. How many times have I shouted, "How many times do I have to tell you to clean up after yourselves? What do you think I am, a free maid? Pick up your toys or I swear, I'll give them to D.I.! Who spilled this milk and just left it there? Nobody in this house appreciates anything I do! Nobody move until this house is spic and span, I mean it! What's wrong with you people, do you think you're just going to sit there while I do all the work?"

You get the picture. It isn't pretty, is it?

A messy house does not have to be a punishment. It can be one of life's joys. But there's no joy like that on a Sunday morning when the house is in order and no one is shouting, "Where's my other shoe? Who took my scriptures? Didn't there used to be three goldfish in the bowl?"

There are days when I fear I will not survive—and my family might not survive me. The trick is to keep our everyday messes, the little ones as well as the big ones, in perspective. Look at the big picture and look for little ways to endure.

My Grandma Sorenson epitomized endurance. She was twenty years old when she married my grandfather in the Manti temple. A year later Grandpa, at the age of twenty-two, was called to be bishop of a brand-new ward. The gospel meant everything to them and they vowed to raise their children in faith and fortitude.

When Grandpa was released as bishop he was called as ward choir director. He loved music and was thrilled with his calling. He was a giant of a man, calloused and toned by hard work and the scorching sun, but a beautiful piece of music would make tears run unashamedly down his cheeks. It was this side of her husband that Grandma loved best

For years he magnified his calling with the choir. Because he did such a good job, the choir's exceptional ability was brought to the attention of the music department at Church headquarters. The choir, led by my proud grandfather, was invited to sing in General Conference! They had nearly a year to prepare and they did not waste one practice session.

Then an incident happened where my grandfather's pride was injured. (That's a sermon for another book. This story is about Grandma and how she endured as her husband went from wounded to worse.) He became bitter and stayed away from church. He began working on Sundays, and soon he started taking his sons to the farm with him.

Grandma was a woman of quiet dignity and dogged determination; she continued steady and true to the course she had set and the covenants she had made. She endured trials much messier than a dusty house. I don't think I could have endured watching my own husband keep my children away from church. I can only imagine her heartbreak, yet the shared reflection her children have of those years was the unfailing love she showed to both her husband and her children.

Every morning it was Grandma who got up and turned the dining-room chairs around so that the family would pray together. She saw that her children paid tithing. She walked to church every Sunday and served faithfully in each calling that came her way. While cleaning the house, she taught her daughters gospel principles. Today, her example continues to teach me.

It was years before my grandfather finally returned to church. By then, my own father, along with some of his siblings, had fallen away from the faith. Grandma never did. Even when things got messy, she was there to clean up. To love unconditionally. To trust God that He would watch after her children.

I remember going to visit Grandma when I was almost grown. She was worried about me because I wasn't a member of the Church. She bore her testimony to me, and though I can't recall her words, I will never forget the feeling of power that was in the room when that sprite of a woman looked me in the eye and promised, "It is true. It's all true."

I was in high school when Grandma died. Grandpa had passed away exactly two years before—after more than sixty years of marriage. Talk about endurance! When I was in college I decided to write her life story. My uncles shared an incident with me that best illustrates the kind of woman, the kind of mother, Grandma was. Two of her sons had moved away from home, joined the army, and had grown to be real men. One day they came home to visit their mother. They enjoyed a home-cooked meal and an afternoon of reminiscing. When they were ready to leave, one of my uncles reached for his jacket. As he did, a package of cigarettes fell out, rolling one by one at Grandma's feet.

Both uncles, clearly guilty, fell to their knees and scrambled to retrieve those cigarettes. "Mother never said a word," my uncle told me. "She just watched as we knelt like fools at her feet. I'll never forget the shame or the regret at seeing the pain and disappointment on Mother's face. After that, I never smoked again."

Thank you, Grandma, for teaching me how to mother.

I wish she were here so I could thank her in person. We all need to feel appreciated in order to keep a proper perspective. "The blessing of nurturing children and caring for a husband often is intermingled with many routine tasks. But you do all of these things willingly because you are a woman. Generally you have no idea of how truly wonderful and capable you are, how very much appreciated and loved, or how desperately needed, for most men don't tell you as completely and as often as needed" (Richard G. Scott, "The Joy of Living the Great Plan of Happiness," *Ensign*, Nov. 1996, 73).

With no appreciation, cleaning the house can never be more than a chore. When we feel appreciated, the chore becomes an act of love.

Yes, there are days on end when I feel like I go a hundred miles an hour to get nowhere. I clean a room, turn around, and it looks like it's never met the vacuum cleaner. I raise my voice, I make demands, I play the martyr.

But I'm getting smarter. I don't clean the house by myself anymore. I enlist the aid of my children, sometimes one-on-one, and sometimes my husband gives the command and we all fall in line. Any one of those times is a good time to talk about the gospel of Jesus Christ. It's good news. And the good news is that "out of small things proceedeth that which is great" (D&C 64:33). Out of a rotten potato comes a lesson about giving thanks. We cannot underestimate the value of the work we do as mothers. President J. Reuben Clark said,

"May God . . . give you the vision of the true homemaker, that you will be able to save by this course, not alone Zion, but the world. And that is your destiny . . . to save the world" (*Relief Society Magazine*, Dec. 1949, 798).

We have endured many things. Spilled grape juice on white carpet. Wedding rings flushed down toilets. Dog vomit on the new sofa. Those are small messes in a world that is really messed up.

May we remember that. May we remember and find the strength through our faith to be able to endure all things, including the daily messes that are just that—messes. I love this quote: "Keep an eternal perspective, especially when you think that diapers and night feedings will never end. You're doing what the Lord wants you to do and you will be blessed" (in Ezra Taft Benson, "The Honored Place of Woman," *Ensign*, Nov. 1981, 104).

From a photo in a frame that needs dusting, itself a lesson in the treasures of genealogy, shines the smile of my grandmother, a woman who whispers to me now that yes, I can endure, and yes, it is worth it. Because with every diaper we change, every dish we wash, every floor we mop, we are "laying the foundation of a great work" (D&C 64:33).

There is none greater.

CHAPTER FOUR

The Lies That Bind

And he became Satan, yea, even the devil, the father of all lies, to deceive and to blind men, and to lead them captive at his will, even as many as would not hearken unto my voice.

—*Moses 4: 4*

A few years ago a book was touted as a guide to genuine spirituality. It promised to fine-tune our souls, to teach women to tap into their innate compass for higher directive. A million copies had already sold, and I stood in line to buy mine. I read the best-seller. Because there was so much good in it, I almost overlooked one short sentence. But there it was: one succinct lie that read simply, "While there is no actual devil . . ."

I nearly dropped the book. What? *No actual devil?*

The author was wrong. Dead wrong. I know it. You know it. There is a devil. Satan is real. Ancient as well as modern revelation testifies of our archenemy. "The contention in heaven was—Jesus said there would be certain souls that would not be saved; and the devil said he could save them all, and laid his plans before the grand council, who gave their vote in favor of Jesus Christ. So the devil rose up in rebellion against God, and was cast down, with all who put up their heads for him" (*Teachings of the Prophet Joseph Smith,* 357).

In a vision to Moses, the Lord revealed: "And he became Satan, yea, even the devil, the father of all lies, to deceive and to blind men, and to lead them captive at his will, even as many as would not hearken unto my voice" (Moses 4:4).

Satan is real and I wanted to shout it from the rooftops. I wanted to write the TV networks, the publisher, the author, and declare what the First Presidency had defined with power and precision: "(Satan) goes by many names and . . . is working under such perfect disguise that many do not recognize either him or his methods. There is no crime he would not commit, no debauchery he would not set up, no plague he would not send, no heart he would not break, no life he would not take, no soul he would not destroy. He comes as a thief in the night; he's a wolf in sheep's clothing (*Improvement Era*, 45:761).

Make no mistake. Evil is alive and thriving in these latter days, and we mothers are in the battle for our very salvation. Brigham Young warned, "The men and women who desire to obtain seats in the celestial kingdom will find that they must battle with the enemy of all righteousness every day" (Brigham Young, *Journal of Discourses*, 11:14). No wonder we're so tired.

It is not in our nature, not in our plan of happiness, to sit in the celestial kingdom alone; we want each member of our family with us. What was the first thing Lehi did after partaking of the fruit of the tree of life? "As I partook of the fruit thereof it filled my soul with exceedingly great joy; wherefore, I began to be desirous that my family should partake of it also . . . I cast my eyes round about, that perhaps I might discover my family also. . . ." (1 Ne. 8:12–13).

Sisters, we are engaged in a battle to save ourselves and to protect our families. We did not seek this combat, but neither can we shun it. We mothers are dual targets. Satan does not stalk just us; his scope is sighted on our children also—and when he aims, he means to kill.

Please don't flee in fear. Fear is the absence of faith. This is not a message of darkness or despair. It is a message of light and total faith. Satan cannot kill us, cannot even wound us if we learn how to recognize and avoid evil. Note that I did not say "battle evil" because we cannot allow ourselves to engage in any combat with evil. Rather, we follow the Savior's example and rebuke evil. Rather than entertaining or engaging in evil, we recognize it and avoid it.

Shortly after our daughter received her driver's license, she brought the family car home with a pronounced dent in the front fender. I waited, expecting her to explain, but she remained mute as she went on her merry way.

I waited and waited. Days passed until I could wait no more. "What happened to the car?" I asked. Her face went blank.

"What do you mean?"

"I mean the fender. There's a giant dent in it."

She looked dumfounded, her jaw dropped nearly to her knees, and she said in the same breath, "I didn't do it!"

With a little guidance from me, we went out to inspect the car together. She pretended she didn't even know where the dent was, but I saw her eyes stray right to the inverted V.

"Whoever was driving had to hit something pretty hard to make a dent like that."

"Well, it wasn't me," she said.

I gave her the look. You know the one; it's meant to melt a daughter's heart into confession. Even when I narrowed my eyes to slits and shot red laser beams from them, my daughter did not confess. I was tempted to offer her a more up-close-and-personal inspection of the damage, but with patience and silence, very uncharacteristic of me, I said nothing, did nothing. That's not entirely true: I prayed. It's the most effective defense a mother has against evil.

It took a few days for her to come to me and admit, "You know that dent in the car?"

"Yeah."

"Well, maybe, just maybe, I *do* remember driving into a cement post in the school parking lot."

I had to swallow the bitter words that sprang to the tip of my tongue and replace them with, "I'd think you'd remember a bump like that."

She dissolved in tears. "Mom, I lied to you; I am so sorry."

"I know," I said, embracing her.

She sniffled and backed away. "You knew I was lying?"

"I knew."

The fender was only bent metal. It could be repaired. How do you repair a damaged spirit? Only through recognition, sincere remorse, and true repentance.

Once forgiveness was sought and granted, through teary red eyes my daughter asked, "Mom, how do you always know when you are being lied to?"

That, dear Sisters, is the question. How can we know when we are being lied to by the greatest liar of all?

The answer to combating such falsehoods is found within the pages of the scriptures.

> That which the Spirit testifies unto you even so I would that ye would do in all holiness of heart, walking uprightly before me, considering the end of your salvation, doing all things with prayer and thanksgiving, that ye may not be seduced by evil spirits, or doctrines of devils, or the commandments of men; for some are of men, and others of devils.
>
> Wherefore, beware lest ye are deceived; and that ye may not be deceived seek ye earnestly the best gifts, always remembering for what they are given;
>
> For verily I say unto you, they are given for the benefit of those who love me . . . (D&C 46:7–9).

Just as we recognize Jesus for light and truth, we can and must recognize the adversary by darkness and deceit. When I was a young woman questioning the Church, a professor at BYU told me, "You can know if your inspiration is from heaven or hell by deciding in which direction it points. If you are being prompted to do good, you are led by divine revelation. If your advice admonishes you to do harm, then you're led by the host of hell."

Alma said it this way: "For I say unto you that whatsoever is good cometh from God, and whatsoever is evil cometh from the devil" (Alma 5:40).

I thought discernment was simple until I tried to differentiate between every decision in my life. Not all decisions are clearly marked *good* and *evil.* It reminds me of a painting we have in our home entitled *Noah's Dilemma.* There stands Noah by his completed ark, the sky is ominous, and the perplexed prophet is surrounded by animals of all kinds—*three* of each species. Three little bunnies, three little ducks, three precious porcupines, all pleading, "Noah, choose me, choose me!" It's an expression that pretty much sums up our decision dilemmas.

Sometimes we are required to choose between good and good. Other times Satan just makes evil *look* good. He's not called the great imposter for nothing.

As daughters who love our Father and our Savior, Satan bombards us with a barrage of lies. The list is endless, but here are a few that he directs frequently and ferociously at women, particularly mothers.

I'm not lying. This is the one lie that all mothers are familiar with; it goes hand in hand with the "I didn't do it" denial. When you hear that dark voice whisper that he is not lying, remember that not all lies are verbalized. Elder Marvin J. Ashton observed, "Not often do students remember for 24 hours very many words taught by their teachers. Yet 50 years later some former students recall with lasting appreciation the words one teacher had her class repeat at the beginning of each day. Every school morning this rather unpretentious, plain, wise lady implanted the meaning of honesty into our minds by having us recite, 'A lie is any communication given to another with the intent to deceive'" ("This Is No Harm," *Ensign,* May 1982, 9).

This is the angle the sinister serpent played when he approached Mother Eve in the Garden. Satan asked, "Yea, hath God said, Ye shall not eat of every tree of the garden?" (Gen. 3:1).

Eve replied, "We may eat of the fruit of the trees of the garden: But of the fruit of the tree which is in the midst of the garden, God hath said, Ye shall not eat of it, . . . lest ye die" (Gen. 3:2–3).

Satan, in a spirit of deception and defiance, responded, "Ye shall not surely die" (Gen. 3:4). Here, he distorted the truth, denied the decree of God, and introduced doubt about Deity. And thus, Satan became the father of lies.

The closer a lie is to the truth, the more deadly it is. And Satan does not aim to merely frighten. His army is well trained and his arsenal is well stocked, and both are aimed right at us.

No one has the right to tell you what to do. We all have a little rebel in us and don't like to be "told" what we should do. Yet somebody better tell the devil what to do and what not to do. We have that power. "All beings who have bodies have power over those who have not. The devil has no power over us only as we permit him. The moment we revolt at anything which comes from God, the devil takes power" (*Teachings of the Prophet Joseph Smith*, 181).

Commandments are for our good. Our growth. "God loves us; the devil hates us. God wants us to have a fullness of joy as He has. The devil wants us to be miserable as he is. God gives us commandments to bless us. The devil would have us break these commandments to curse us" (Ezra Taft Benson, "The Great Commandment—Love the Lord," *Ensign*, May 1988, 6).

God *does* have a right to tell us what to do. He is our Father, and He loves us with an unspeakable, unconditional love. He has every right and if we will but heed His counsel, our lives will always be better.

Think about it. As parents, our wisdom and experience are limited, yet they are greater than that of our children. So when we advise them, we do it to guide and protect them, to spare them unnecessary suffering. We get upset when they set aside our counsel and say, "I'll do it my way."

But what do we do when our Father advises us?

Next time Satan whispers to your ego, to the rebel in you, stand tall and straight and say aloud, "As for me and my house . . ." (Josh. 24:15) When you do, Satan's temptation loses its power. Paint it on the walls, carve it in the woodwork, shout it from your rooftop . . . believe it!

You are insignificant in the grand scheme of things. How many times have I fallen for this one? For most of my life I've believed that my contribution held very little value. Even with a testimony of the gospel, I failed to really believe that I mattered. I voiced those beliefs to the detriment of myself and my children. I was deceived into believing that all my self-disparaging remarks attested to my humility. I was wrong. I was self-centered instead of Christ-centered. A quote from Erma Bombeck gave me a new perspective: "When I get to the other side and stand before Jesus, when he asks me what I did with my talent, I'll say, 'I have no talent, I used every bit you gave me.'"

And so began a change in me that Alma referred to as "mighty." I knelt before the Lord and repented. "Whatever I am, whatever I have, all my strengths and all my weaknesses, they're all yours, Lord."

I don't know what I expected. What I received was a peaceful, loving, inaudible assurance that my offering had been accepted.

Little sins wash away easily. This is another lie that mothers should recognize right away. One teeny-tiny little stain on the front of a white Sunday shirt can ruin the whole shirt. (Unless it can be creatively camouflaged by a jacket, a tie, or a giant *I Am a Child of God* sticker.)

There are no little sins. The road to repentance does not run downhill. Sins are snares that trap us, and when repeated often enough, they bind us tight. We are stronger than earthly temptation, but not when left on our own. Fortunately, we are never left on our own. "I am the way, the truth, and the life," said the Savior (John 14:6). His strength is sufficient to free us.

President Boyd K. Packer taught: "Lucifer in clever ways manipulates our choices, deceiving us about sin and consequences. He, and his angels with him, tempt us to be unworthy, even wicked. But he cannot, in all eternity he cannot, with all his power he cannot completely destroy us; not without our own consent ("Atonement, Agency, Accountability," *Ensign*, May 1988, 71).

"In a fictional letter, the master devil, Screwtape, instructs the apprentice devil Wormwood, who is in training to become a more experienced devil: 'You will say that these are very small sins; and doubtless, like all young tempters, you are anxious to be able to report spectacular wickedness. . . . It does not matter how small the sins are, provided that their cumulative effect is to edge the man away from the Light and out into the Nothing. . . . Indeed, the safest road to Hell is the gradual one—the gentle slope, soft underfoot, without sudden turnings, without milestones, without signposts' (C.S. Lewis, *The Screwtape Letters*, 56). (James E. Faust, "The Great Imitator," *Ensign*, Nov 1987, 34).

You are not capable. You *are* capable. This lie has been told so many times it should be worn see-through thin. The engineer of your design was not practicing; you are not an experimental model.

You are not worthy. This lie always follows the *You are not capable* lie. What irks me is how Satan convinces us to sin and then turns right around and condemns us for the sin he's coerced us into committing. First he leads us, then he leaves us. Remember, that once you serve Satan and do his dirty work, you're on your own (see Alma 30:60).

If you have sinned and are not worthy of the blessing you seek, don't listen to Satan. Listen to the one who says, "Come unto me . . ." (Matt. 11:28).

Repent.

Get worthy.

If you try, you will fail. This is the lie that Satan tells us whenever we are on the verge of accomplishing great good. If you are thinking of going on a mission, he'll tell you what a lousy missionary you'll be. If you are called to teach, he'll tell you no one will pay attention. He will make you feel small and stupid. Don't believe him. This lie, like most lies, is a lie based on fear. I don't know a mother who is not afraid—afraid she'll undernourish her babies, afraid she'll overindulge her teenagers. Afraid she'll take a perfect little soul and cause it irreparable harm.

Fear feeds on fear. Plato understood Satan's greatest fear—that we will see through his lies. "We can easily forgive a child who is afraid of the dark. The real tragedy of life is when men are afraid of the light."

The light to do right is within us. It is the same illumination that came from the One who spoke without fear, but with complete faith. "Here am I, send me" (Abr. 3:27).

Nelson Mandella echoed a supporting insight. "Our deepest fear is not that we are inadequate. Our deepest fear is that we are powerful beyond measure. It is our light, not our darkness, that most frightens us. We ask ourselves, who am I to be brilliant, gorgeous, talented, and fabulous? Actually, who are you not to be? You are a child of God. Your playing small doesn't serve the world. There is nothing enlightened about shrinking so that other people won't feel insecure around you."

Let this truth be manna to our hungry, trembling souls. We are all afraid. It's time we step forward and do it—afraid or not!

It can wait. "It" is whatever the Spirit whispers for us to do. We can't be lax or lazy; we can't even listen to the evil one. The Lord's command cannot wait. Make haste to do good. Like David, we must run to the battlefield when called.

When we are prompted to serve, we must serve. If the Spirit whispers that someone is in need, we must go to them. We can't wait to do good. It is the Lord's work and now is the time to thrust in the sickle and begin.

"Eat, drink, and be merry, for tomorrow we die" (2 Ne. 28:7). This is such a familiar lie we should all recognize it for what it's worth—a swift trip to the basement of eternity.

The Lord wants us to be happy, even joyous. Indulging in excesses will never lead to anything but misery. You sin—you suffer. "True happiness in this life and the life to come is found in keeping the commandments of God. ' . . . you shall live by every word that proceedeth forth from the mouth of God (D&C 84:44)" (David B. Haight, "Power of Evil," *Ensign*, July 1973, 54).

You shouldn't bother God with little things. When Satan tells you this whopper, tell him your Heavenly Father is never bothered when we approach Him through prayer. Never, ever. We are His children. He loves us. This was best demonstrated in the book of Mark. Jesus and His disciples were leaving Jericho when they encountered a blind man named Bartimaeus, who sat at the side of the highway begging. Apparently, he knew of Jesus for the scriptures tell us, "when he heard that it was Jesus of Nazareth, he began to cry out, and say, Jesus, thou Son of David, have mercy on me."

Immediately, many went to the man and told him to "hold his peace," or in other words, don't bother Jesus.

But the beggar didn't listen to them, just as we should not listen to Satan. Instead, "he cried the more a great deal, Thou Son of David, have mercy on me."

His disciples wanted to press on, but Jesus stopped and called forth the man.

The man cast away his coat and struggled toward the Master.

"What wilt thou that I should do unto thee?" Jesus asked.

"The blind man said unto him, Lord, that I might receive my sight.

"And Jesus said unto him, Go thy way; thy faith hath made thee whole. And immediately he received his sight, and followed Jesus in the way" (Mark 10:46–52).

It wasn't God. We've all been blessed with answered prayers. Tiny miracles. Finding a lost set of keys. Saying just the right thing when a child needs counsel. Whenever heaven intervenes on your behalf, make a record, tell your loved ones, testify, and remember. If you don't, Satan will convince you that what happened would have happened anyway, and it had nothing to do with divine assistance. "You only need to rely on yourself," Satan says.

We know better. William Temple said it this way, "When I pray, coincidences happen, and when I don't, they don't" (*Inspiring Quotes*, 161).

The list could go on and on, and it does, but by addressing some of the most popular lies, we can hopefully identify others. We can listen and obey the voice of all truth and turn deaf ears to the voice of deceit.

Mormon tells us, "For every man receiveth wages of him whom he listeth to obey" (Alma 3:27).

May we listen to the Lord. Just as we know Jesus by His light, we can know Satan by his lies. It matters not that Satan comes in "perfect disguise," we can know him we can recognize him, and we can reject him.

"By every possible means he seeks to darken the minds of men and then offers them falsehood and deception in the guise of truth.

Satan is a skillful imitator, and as genuine gospel truth is given the world in ever-increasing abundance, so he spreads the counterfeit coin of false doctrine. . . . [As] 'the father of lies' he has . . . become, through the ages of practice in his nefarious work, such an adept that were it possible he would deceive the very elect" (Joseph F. Smith in Daniel H. Ludlow, *Latter-day Prophets Speak*, 20–21).

Mothers in Zion are elect. Our children are among the most valiant of all God's spirit children. He has not sent us to this earth to be tested so that we fail. Paul admonished us to be vigilant "lest Satan should get an advantage of us: for we are not ignorant of his devices" (2 Cor. 2:11). We are not ignorant, we are not alone, and we are not without resources. The Lord reminds us of His love and concern. And again, I will give unto you a pattern in all things, that ye may not be deceived; for Satan is abroad in the land" (D&C 52:14).

There is a pattern to Satan's lies. Each and every one of them tugs us downward, away from heaven and farther from happiness.

We are engaged in a battle of good versus evil. As long as we are on the Lord's side, we are empowered with a strength stronger than evil, a hope brighter than darkness. To safeguard our children and strengthen our homes, we must distinguish between Satan and our Savior. We must teach our loved ones that "all things which are good cometh of God; and that which is evil cometh of the devil; for the devil is an enemy unto God, . . . and inviteth and enticeth to sin" (Moro. 7:12).

It is the sweetest manna to a mother's soul to know that with God, her strength is the strength of ten, her wisdom the wisdom of heaven. Our best efforts will be rewarded, for the Lord has assured, "Keep all the commandments and covenants by which ye are bound; and I will cause the heavens to shake for your good, and Satan shall tremble and Zion shall rejoice upon the hills and flourish" (D&C 35: 24).

Doesn't that sound like a great place to raise a family?

CHAPTER FIVE

Balance Your Life in Three Seconds Flat

Thou shalt thank the Lord thy God in all things.
—Doctrine & Covenants 59:7

Not many of life's lessons are simple or painless. This one is. It can balance our teetering existence in three seconds flat.

Sound intriguing?

It is.

Sound easy?

It is.

When I give this presentation at women's workshops, the question always arises: Why are so many of us, women with testimonies of the gospel, out of balance, teetering dangerously close to—sometimes over—the edge of discouragement, depression, despair? Because we forget to keep one of the most important commandments given in this last dispensation. "Thou shalt thank the Lord thy God in *all* things" (D&C 59:7).

Three seconds.

Three words.

Think to thank. Or, if you prefer to sing it, *Count your blessings.*

It is at this point in the presentation that women begin to sigh audibly, to roll their eyes, and shift uncomfortably in their seats, wishing they were down the hall in the workshop entitled, "Replicating the City of Nauvoo out of Tootsie Rolls."

It is easy to dismiss the simple exercise for something more complex, perhaps *Seven Secrets, Twelve Steps, One Hundred and One Ways.* We have somehow trapped ourselves into thinking that the best way is always the hardest way. But the Savior's way is never complex or confusing. The path is straight, the way is narrow. "Come follow me," He said, and He meant it. That does not mean living the gospel is easy. It isn't. It isn't meant to be. But we do not have to navigate our way through life alone.

Christ is our leader, our director, our guide. He knows the way because He's walked the path before us. He exemplifies a life of living gratitude, and promises endless rewards for those whose hearts are grateful. "And he who receiveth all things with thankfulness shall be made glorious; and the things of this earth shall be added unto him, even an hundred fold, yea, more" (D&C 78:19).

Three seconds.

Three words.

Think to Thank.

President Thomas S. Monson coined the phrase and explained, "In these three words are the finest capsule course for a happy marriage, a formula for enduring friendship, and a pattern for personal happiness" (*Pathways to Perfection,* 1973, 254).

A grateful heart is a happy heart. It pumps a life-sustaining manna that feeds the body and spirit. My life was completely and totally transformed by this simple, three-second lesson.

Keep in mind as I bear my testimony to these truths that I was not raised a Latter-day Saint. I was brought up in a vehemently anti-Mormon environment. My father died before I started kindergarten. My mother was an alcoholic, so I zig-zagged between foster care providers. In spite of her addiction and all of the ramifications, I adored my mother. I wanted desperately to stay with her permanently, but her life was out of balance. Mother was unable to care for herself, let alone me.

Some people tried to help; others took advantage and brought only harm. My heart clenched tight, a fist ready for a fight. I found myself cynical and suspicious, not knowing who to trust, so I trusted no one—except maybe God. I'd been taught that He existed, that I was His child, that He had power to change everything. I prayed with the faith of a child, fervent and true, that God would change my mother. I asked him to "fix" her so we could stay together.

Then Mother died.

In the turbulent teenage years that followed, let's just say I became an *un*holy terror. I was hurt, angry, and bitter. If we will let Him, the Lord can take what's bitter in our lives and make it better, but I didn't know that then. A broken heart can be mended by the Master's touch, but I didn't know that then. I had much for which to be grateful, but I didn't know that then.

All I knew then was self-pity and pain. Juvenile Detention centers were crowded and incapable of catering to a tempestuous temperament like mine. Relatives shut doors in my face. Foster families locked me out. I don't blame anyone. Their homes were refuges and I was the storm.

I share this experience with you only because I want you to know that the Lord's arms are long enough and strong enough to reach down and lift us out of any pit in which we find ourselves. It doesn't matter if we are thrown in like Joseph, or if we dug our own pit, like I did.

Gratitude is a divine principle that elevates. In the midst of adversity and pain we can find anointing and peace if we seek out reasons to be grateful. I was miserable because I was ungrateful and unaware of all of my blessings. I was miserable and I wanted everyone around me to be miserable too.

An unsuspecting uncle and aunt were charitable enough to take me into their home and into their lives. They also took me to church—to a Mormon Church.

Life in a little Utah town founded by the faith and hard work of pioneers was just what this city girl's heart needed. That, and a bishop who met me at the chapel door, grinning. His big burly hand reached out to clasp mine. "Welcome, Sister Toni, this is where you belong."

I had never belonged *any*where.

The bishop's name was Cecil Bown. The man was a walking lightbulb—always warm, always glowing. Forever grateful. That was way back in the olden days before block meetings. Sunday School was held on Sunday mornings. Sacrament meetings were held at night. The building wasn't really a church; it was an old rock pioneer structure in disrepair, without proper heating and no air conditioning at all. Bats swooped through the rafters during nighttime sacrament services.

I had attended various big-city churches with my mother. The buildings and ministers were impressive. There was no comparison. Cecil Bown and the rickety Mormon Church won hands down. They had peace. They had love. They had fun.

Why? Because they chose to be grateful for all they had instead of whining about what they didn't have.

"We're grateful for the bats," Bishop Bown joked one night, "especially during high council meetings; their presence keeps our audience awake."

I hadn't lived in that community very long when one morning my uncle woke me up and said, "We're headed off to Central America—in an hour."

"Central America?"

"That's right. Pack your bags."

My heart sank. I would not admit it, but I was just beginning to feel comfortable, at home, and at peace with the Mormons. I did not want to be uprooted again.

"I can't go to Central America. I don't speak Spanish," I protested.

"Don't worry," said my uncle, "you're not going. We're dropping you off at the bishop's house on our way out of town."

Thirty minutes later I was standing on the front doorstep of the Bown residence, paper grocery bag of my belongings in hand. They lived on a dairy farm and had five sons. I think Sister Bown was as surprised as I was.

"Welcome," said Bishop Bown.

"Welcome," said his wife.

My heart, that was just beginning to open, slammed shut. This wasn't church. This was just another foster home where people said, "Welcome," but they didn't mean it.

I was wrong. The Bown family was different. The same warm feeling that filled the church filled their home. They included me in their lives. Everyone got up early in the morning, milked cows, did chores, ate together, and then we kids rode the bus eight miles to school. Sister Bown cooked meals and baked her own bread. She had a sewing machine and knew how to thread it. Homework was done at the kitchen table. There were always chores waiting to be done, calves waiting to be fed, and cows waiting to be milked. Enough work to wilt a city kid.

They were happy. They were grateful. At night they listed all their blessings and said, "Thanks" to the Lord in prayer.

Incorporating me in their daily routines wasn't easy, but the Bown family didn't send me away like other foster families had. They included me in family home evenings. After a few weeks, Bishop

Bown handed me the manual and told me that the next week's lesson was mine. They included me in family prayer. They taught me how to pray. At Christmas time they bought me a clock radio—the only gift anyone besides my mother had ever given me.

It was the Bowns' example of patience, love, and gratitude that gave me the foundation for a new life. It wasn't easy, and I was far, far from perfect, but I *was* truly thankful for my new life.

But thankfulness is only a cousin to gratitude. A thankful heart sings and dances. A grateful heart goes to work. *Think to thank* is the exercise that pumps love through every heart. It is life-sustaining manna.

A lifetime later, when I was the mother of four healthy, relatively happy children, I knelt beside my bed and poured out my heart's deepest emotions. "Father, my heart is so full. Please give me a chance to show Thee the depth of my gratitude."

What I did not realize is that I was praying for the greatest challenge of my life. Soon after that the telephone rang. A friend of mine was on the other end informing us of a baby who needed a home. My husband did not hesitate. I *could* not hesitate, not when there had been people like my uncle and aunt and the Bown family willing to take me in.

The next morning, under very unconventional circumstances, we were blessed with a baby boy. His birth mother loved him dearly, but was not capable of caring for him. He came with no medical records, no birth certificate. His frail little body was covered in open sores and scars. He had the muscle tone of cooked spaghetti, the disposition of a screech owl. Our new son's only response to my motherly touch was to cry louder.

No, no, no, I told myself, this is not how it's supposed to be. I'm a seasoned mother; when I hold him he's supposed to stop crying. He's supposed to fit right into our family. He's supposed to love me because I love him.

He didn't. And something inside of me went askew.

Our son wanted nothing to do with his new family and could not be consoled. He screamed for hours on end, slept fitfully, and woke to resume his wailing. What's more, our son is black, and people from every race seemed to have something to say about our pasty Scandinavian family adopting a child of color.

The rest of the family adapted. Not me. I felt bewildered and guilty. I searched for something I could do to find peace.

I did not think to thank.

Months passed. Medical bills mounted. My patience and energy dwindled. I was spiritually malnourished—for one reason only. I failed to show up at the Lord's table. I told myself I was too tired. Too busy.

What I expected to be a season of happiness became an endless stretch of darkness and despair. Our son seldom smiled and never made eye contact. I wasn't much happier. He downed bottle after bottle of nutrient-rich formula. His body refused to gain weight or strength.

I did not think to thank. My focus was on everything that was wrong; I was blinded to all the things that were right.

I did not think to thank. I was resentful and judgmental. I was indescribably tired. My prayers resounded with whys and woes. No wonder I struggled in the undertow.

An entire year passed. Our lives swelled with love for our baby, but he still weighed fourteen pounds, though he ate like a lumberjack. He could barely lift his head, had use of only one leg, and could not make intelligible sounds. The pediatric specialist assigned to us advised, "Put him in an institution where he can be cared for properly. Your son will never walk. Never talk. Never even crawl."

I did not think to thank. I was too tired and too discouraged. What more could I do?

One night while we both slept momentarily, I dreamt of another struggling family. The next day I read their story in the book of Luke. Mary and Martha loved their brother Lazarus but he fell ill and died. The sisters, in their grief, reached out to the same Lord I should have been reaching out to.

Jesus loved Lazarus and his sisters. He knew that Lazarus had died that His own divinity might be made manifest. He "abode two days still in the same place where he was" (John 11:6).

Just waiting for a miracle sometimes makes it all that more miraculous when it does occur. By the time Jesus arrived, Lazarus had been dead four days! That's about how I felt.

The faithful sisters mourned for their brother, but did not doubt the power of the Savior. Martha chose an attitude of gratitude. "I know, that even now, whatsoever thou wilt ask of God, God will give it thee.

"Jesus saith unto her, Thy brother shall rise again" (John 11:22–23).

Martha did not understand the full ramifications, the glorious good news of the gospel He was teaching. "I know that he shall rise again in the resurrection at the last day.

Jesus said unto her, I am the resurrection, and the life: he that believeth in me, though he were dead, yet shall he live: And whosoever liveth and believeth in me shall never die. Believest thou this?

She saith unto him, Yea, Lord: I believe " (John 11:24–27).

Mary shared the same sentiment, though she too did not fully comprehend.

Jesus did. And he wept.

Spectators assumed Christ cried because He had lost His beloved friend. But Lazarus was not lost. When they came to the cave where Lazarus lay, "Jesus said, Take ye away the stone. . . .

"Then they took away the stone from the place where the dead was laid. And Jesus lifted up his eyes, and said, Father, I thank thee that thou hast heard me" (John 11:39, 41).

I paid close attention. Jesus was offering thanks *before* the miracle. He was grateful for His Father's faith in Him, He was grateful for His friends, for this opportunity to testify of His mission. I knew that faith preceded the miracle, but gratitude? What a lesson!

"And when he thus had spoken, he cried with a loud voice, Lazarus, come forth. And he that was dead came forth" (John 11:43–44).

I sought out a quiet place where I prayed more fervently and faithfully than ever. Funny thing is, I spoke no words, not even in my mind. I simply and desperately opened my heart and begged the Lord to read it.

I wanted to know what was wrong with me. Why was the joy gone from my life? Mothering this needy baby was not a burden; it was a blessing. I loved my son. I loved the gospel. What was wrong with me?

I wasn't asking that my son be made whole. I knew better. Our first baby died before we could bring him home from the hospital. I was asking for a new direction, a new stamina, a new hope. I wanted to rise above the mire.

Think to thank was the prompting my spirit received.

An attitude of gratitude was the real miracle I sought. I prayed to be grateful for all that my son *was*, not resentful for all that he was *not.* It was hearing my own sermon preached at me! So simple. How could I have missed so much?

President Joseph F. Smith did not sugarcoat my sin. "One of the greatest sins of which the inhabitants of the earth are guilty to-day, is the sin of ingratitude" (*Journal of Discourses*, 25:52). The scriptures leave no room for misinterpretation: "And in nothing doth man offend God, or against none is his wrath kindled, save those who confess not his hand in *all* things, and obey not his commandments" (D&C 59:21, emphasis added).

Gratitude is not an optional commandment. "And ye must give thanks unto God in the Spirit for whatsoever blessing ye are blessed with" (D&C 46:32).

I repented and never have I been so grateful for Christ's atoning sacrifice. He atoned for my ingratitude. He allowed me the chance to change. I began to seek until I could see reasons to give thanks. My eyes were opened to tiny miracles (is there really such a things as a tiny miracle?) that had been there all along, but my ingratitude had kept me from recognizing them. Tiny miracles like waking up to have a whole new day to spend. Tiny miracles like a baby's smile, a coo, and his first real laugh. The first time my son's eyes met mine and did not look away was a day to rejoice.

"This is the day which the LORD hath made; we will rejoice and be glad in it" (Ps. 118:24). Being grateful is being aware of the blessings that surround us. Being grateful is a choice. Elder David B. Haight said, "I hope that we have grateful hearts for the knowledge that we have and the testimonies we have and for the feelings we have" ("Faith, Devotion, and Gratitude," *Ensign*, May 2000, 35).

Silent gratitude doesn't do anyone any good. If we feel gratitude it is important that we voice those feelings. To our Father and His Son, to our loved ones. To the woman who bags our groceries. I bought a journal and began keeping track of all that I had to be grateful for; reviewing it was a sure way of refocusing my life.

The cold winter morning our son was sealed to us in the Salt Lake Temple was the morning I truly began to appreciate the power of the Holy Priesthood.

Not all stories in my life continue in such a hopeful vein. Our son is now enrolled in elementary school. He plays soccer and basketball and can beat me, "hands down" in arm wrestling. He plays tackle football and street hockey with the neighbor kids. He's still shy around strangers, but he talks nonstop around his family.

I share this painfully personal story with you not to focus on my son's incredible strengths or on my countless weaknesses, but to testify that when we think to thank, our lives undergo a radical remodeling. Spiritual feng shui places living foliage where there were dead leaves, gushing water where there was drought, fresh air where there was stench, hope where there was despair. An attitude of gratitude brings energy, encouragement, and excitement.

I am not saying that gratitude in the midst of heartache will heal all things broken. I am saying that a grateful heart mends a lot quicker. It beats a lot stronger. And it is open to inspiration. A grateful heart is an open invitation for continued blessings. To paraphrase King Benjamin, "As soon as you thank God for one blessing—be prepared to receive another one!"

When Dallas was six years old we received another telephone call. Another baby, a son we named Elijah, came into our lives. And this time around, my heart remained grateful. I am blessed among women. I know it. And I thank my Heavenly Father for His grace and goodness.

There are times and trials that tax all of us. But if we can stop, fall to our knees, and pray, "Grant me a heart that beats with gratitude," I promise you your life will be brighter. Elie Wiesel, upon accepting the 1986 Nobel Peace Prize said, "No one is as capable of gratitude as one who has emerged from the kingdom of night."

Our Savior emerged from that kingdom victorious. "In the world ye shall have tribulation," assured Jesus Christ, "but be of good cheer; I have overcome the world" (John 16:33).

He has already done it for us. Why, then, do we think it is required of us to shoulder the weight of the world? To carry burdens we should cast aside? To make installment payments on a debt our Savior has already paid for us?

Think to thank.

Think of one blessing at a time.

Thank the giver of all good things. Even when you think the thing you've been given isn't so good.

Recognize the blessing you have if you expect to be "added upon."

Of all the blessings I am blessed with, the one for which I am most grateful is my testimony. I know I am a daughter of Deity. I know that you are, too. I know that Jesus Christ atoned for my sins—the big ones, the little ones, even the stupid, stupid ones. I know that Joseph Smith really did see and hear God the Father and His Son in a grove of trees. I know that a living prophet leads us today. I know that prayers are heard and answered. I know that my life was changed with a three-second lesson.

Think to thank. May we demonstrate our gratitude by the way we treat each other, by the way we treat ourselves.

In times of want and times of plenty, may we count our blessings—that is, if we can count that high.

CHAPTER SIX

Seven Times Hotter

My God hath been my support; he hath led me
through mine afflictions in the wilderness;
and he hath preserved me upon the waters of the great deep.
——2 Nephi 4:20

I was feeling pretty good about myself, having just survived another hour of exercise class. My tummy was at least a millimeter flatter than it had been an hour previously. Hand in hand with my young son, we walked toward our car through the immense parking lot, maneuvering our way between parked vehicles.

Somewhere between a white Ford Taurus and a minivan filled with Sunbeams, I got stuck. Wedged might be a truer description of my dilemma.

My son, inches ahead of me, cheered me one. "Come on, Mom. You can do it."

"You can do it!" chanted the minivan.

I tried. I inhaled and twisted every which way I could. It was no use. I filled the gap like JELL-O fills a mold.

My son inspected the situation from one end to the other, then posed the million-pound question, "Mom, can you suck it in from the *back*?"

I laughed because that's what I do. And when I laughed I jostled myself free.

Why is it, just when we begin to feel good about the progress we're making, something adverse happens? When we do the right thing isn't life supposed to get easier? No. Only through struggles are we strengthened.

The story of three young Israelite boys, friends of Daniel—Shadrach, Meshach, and Abed-nego—has significant meaning in my life. Israel was besieged by Babylon. Those young Hebrew boys deemed strongest and most capable were kidnapped, ripped away from their homes and families, and taken to serve in the royal court. Shadrach, Meshach, and Abed-nego stood valiant and steadfast, true to their convictions. They passed what I call the "all you can eat buffet test." A royal feast was set before them. The richest entrees, the finest wines. But those boys asked that they be allowed to maintain what I call the Hebrew "pulse" diet—low fat, high fiber. And lots of water to wash down all that manna.

The young men stood fast and true to their convictions. When they were brought before King Nebuchadnezzar, "he found them ten times better than all the magicians and astrologers that were in all his realm" (Dan. 1:20).

Later, when they had earned officership in the royal court, a towering golden image representing King Nebuchadnezzar was cast and it was decreed that on a certain day, at an appointed time, music would signal a time for all to fall down and worship that idol. Anyone who refused would be cast into a fiery furnace.

Shadrach, Meshach, and Abed-nego had already proven their loyalty to their God. In the face not of danger but of death, those young boys stood tall and defiant, true to their convictions.

King Nebuchadnezzar was livid. He vowed to these young men "if . . . ye [will] worship the image which I have made; well: but if ye worship not, ye shall be cast the same hour into the midst of a burning fiery furnace" (Dan. 3:15).

Their response? Unflinching and unwilling to compromise, they replied, "O Nebuchadnezzar, . . . our God whom we serve is able to deliver us from the burning fiery furnace, and he will deliver us." Then came the show of even higher courage. "But if not, be it known unto thee, O king, that we will not serve thy gods, nor worship the golden image" (Dan. 3:16–18).

This is the time when the hand of the Lord came forth to pat those young men on the back, right? To deliver them from harm, hardship, heat?

No.

Not just yet.

Now that they had passed the test, there came a rise in temperature. "Turn up the heat," was Nebuchadnezzar's decree. "Seven times more." (Dan. 3:19).

Seven times hotter than was necessary to incinerate those young boys.

Ever feel like that? Just when you do the right thing for the right reason, your trials get "seven times hotter"?

Those young men stood together, "were bound in their coats, their hosen, and their hats, and their other garments, and were cast into the midst of the burning fiery furnace" by "the most mighty men" in the king's army (Dan. 3:20, 22).

Those same mighty men were slain by the intense heat of the furnace as they cast in Shadrach, Meshach, and Abed-nego. The king looked into the inferno and was astonished. "Did not we cast three men bound into the midst of the fire?" he asked.

"True, O king," came the reply.

But the king's own eyes saw four men, not bound, but loose, "walking in the midst of the fire . . . and the form of the fourth is like the Son of God" (Dan. 3:24–25).

Nebuchadnezzar himself went near to the mouth of the furnace and called forth the young men. They were not even singed. They did not even smell like smoke!

And the king was convinced of the power of the God of Shadrach, Meshach, and Abed-nego. They were granted the right to worship their God. Then the king promoted Shadrach, Meshach, and Abed-nego, in the province of Babylon" (Dan. 3:30).

Consider with me the possibility that trials we go *through* may be preparing us for the promotion God has in store for us. The children of Israel were not permitted to step into the Promised Land until after they had been led *through* the wilderness.

I understand the story of Shadrach, Meshach, and Abed-nego; it has a beginning, a middle, and a glorious ending. The story of the prophet Abinadi is not quite so easy to dissect. Abinadi was steadfast, courageous, and faithful. He too stood defiant before an idolatrous king. When his life was threatened, all Abinadi had to do was retract his testimony to be saved. Instead he vowed, "I will not recall the words which I have spoken unto you concerning this people, for they are true" (Mosiah 17:9).

Three cheers for Abinadi. The flames that surrounded him were powerless to harm him, too—right? Wrong.

If I had written the story of Abinadi, I would have saved him.

But the story is not fiction, and God was the author. The same God that saved Shadrach, Meshach, and Abed-nego stayed his hand and allowed Abinadi to suffer the most horrendous death imaginable.

My question to you is, "Why?"

Why does God intervene to protect one person and allow another to perish? Why does God send a quiver full of children to one woman and leave another wanting woman barren?

Elder Vaughn J. Featherstone tells the following story.

> A young man and his friend were up hiking in the lower foothills near Cody, Wyoming. The friend jumped across a high-power line that was down, but the other young man got tangled in it and was electrocuted. The friend turned and ran all the way back down to where the father lived—and it wasn't a short distance—and told the father that his son had been electrocuted and that he was dead. The father, who was not a young man, ran all the way back up, taking about fifteen minutes. When he got up to where the boy was lying across the wires, he somehow removed the boy from the wires with a board or a large branch. Then he picked his son up in his arms and held him, saying, "In the name of Jesus Christ and by the power and authority of the holy Melchizedek Priesthood, I command you to live." The dead boy opened up his eyes in his father's arms and was taken to the University of Utah Medical Center, where he recovered ("Where Following Him Can Lead Us," *Ensign,* Feb. 1981, 6).

I personally know of another story, eerily similar. Except that the young man, a valiant returned missionary engaged to be married in the temple in a matter of days, did not respond to the command to rise and be made whole.

He died.

Why?

Was one father's faith weaker? One father's priesthood less powerful? Was it the will of the Almighty that one son be spared and another son taken?

If I had the answers to life's hard questions my own life would be different. I don't have the answers, but I do have the faith to know without doubt that God has the answers. President James E. Faust explained why bad things are allowed to happen to good people. "Into every life there come the painful, despairing days of adversity and buffeting. There seems to be a full measure of anguish, sorrow, and often heartbreak for everyone, including those who earnestly seek to do right and be faithful" ("The Refiner's Fire," *Ensign,* May 1979, 53).

Elder Bruce R. McConkie was clear on the trials of mortality:

> It is not, never has been, and never will be the design and purpose of the Lord—however much we seek him in prayer—to answer all our problems and concerns without struggle and effort on our part. This mortality is a probationary estate. . . . We are being tested to see how we will respond in various situations; how we will decide issues; what course we will pursue while we are here walking, not by sight, but by faith ("Why the Lord Ordained Prayer," *Ensign,* Jan. 1976, 11).

Only through faith can we find the peace and assurance that life is not senseless chaos. "Of all our needs, I think the greatest is an increase in faith" said Gordon B. Hinckley ("Lord, Increase Our Faith," *Ensign*, Nov. 1987, 54).

As a child I was taught that there was a God in heaven. I could pray to Him and He would listen. I was taught that the faith of a child could invite angels. When I was seven or eight, I was sent to live in a particularly vile foster home. I prayed that my mother would sober up and come rescue me. She didn't. I was locked in a dark basement where the light bulb was unscrewed from the socket and the windows painted black. I prayed for light. The room remained pitch black. I prayed for protection, but I was not spared abuse. I prayed for a miracle. A miracle never came.

Or did it?

Here I am, alive and able to share with you any scraps of wisdom I've gleaned while going through the trials of life. I suspect I am something like the bumblebee. Mary Kay Ash observed, "Aerodynamically the bumblebee shouldn't be able to fly, but the bumblebee doesn't know that so it goes on flying anyway."

The odds were against me. But heaven was for me. So here I am (shaped very much like a bumblebee), buzzing with enthusiasm about six facts that can increase our faith.

He Knows Your Heart

The singular message I want to reiterate is: *He knows your heart. Heavenly Father knows you and He loves you.* He loves all of us in spite of our faults and flaws. He sees that beneath the color of our highlights lies gray. He knows that without our girdles our tummies are not as flat. He knows our temperaments, that we're not as patient as we want to be. He knows everything about us and still He loves us, not because we have earned His love, but because we are His children.

What other truth and power do we need to succeed in this life? There is no greater power than the love of God. President Ezra Taft Benson taught, "God our Father, Jesus, our Elder Brother and our Redeemer, and the Holy Ghost, the Testator, are perfect. They know us best and love us most and will not leave one thing undone for our eternal welfare" ("The Great Commandment—Love the Lord," *Ensign*, May 1988, 5).

We are loved. May we act like loved, secure children.

Father Has a Plan

Second, God has a plan for our happiness. What a wonderful, warm, and reassuring thing it is to know that the primary objective of the very God of heaven is "the immortality and eternal life of man" (Moses 1:39).

Our Father wants us to be happy. Sometimes I wonder if we really appreciate what that means and how it should affect our lives. The prophet Joseph Smith taught, "Happiness is the object and design of our existence; and will be the end thereof, if we pursue the path that leads to it; and this path is virtue, uprightness, faithfulness, holiness, and keeping all the commandments of God" (*Teachings of the Prophet Joseph Smith*, 255–56).

Faithful people are happy people, regardless of their circumstances. Happiness is a choice, and we have the power to choose the path that leads to true and everlasting happiness. That path is marked by obedience to the commandments. There is no other way.

Adversity Is Not Our Enemy

Adversity is not to be avoided. It is by those who have suffered that the world has been advanced.

I want to get to the Promised Land; I just don't want to go

through the wilderness. Mothers in particular are prone to feel stuck in the wasteland. It's difficult to gauge our progress when sand is blowing in our faces, when desert storms blind us to any progress we might be making. We can't see where we've been, and we can't see where we're going. We have to trust that though we cannot see, there is One who sees for us and can lead the way if we will let Him.

One mother, whose three children were all teenagers, was asked, "Knowing all that you do now, would you still have children?"

"Oh, yes!" she replied. "Sure I would, just not the *same* ones!"

I'm afraid there are moments when we all wonder what it would be like to swap trials with someone else. Not children, just trials. It's not possible. I once spent a whole week offering mine to anyone. Anyone at all. I found no takers, even when I added bags of chocolate.

Our Father knows us. He allows us the unique and particular afflictions that we need in order to grow. "I give unto men weakness that they may be humble" (Ether 12:27). "And inasmuch as they were humble they might be made strong" (D&C 1:28). "Being human," said President Spencer W. Kimball, "we would expel from our lives physical pain and mental anguish and assure ourselves of continual ease and comfort, but if we were to close the doors upon sorrow and distress, we might be excluding our greatest friends and benefactors. Suffering can make saints of people as they learn patience, long-suffering, and self-mastery" (*Faith Precedes the Miracle,* 98).

Our adversities come in different packages and are delivered at different times in our lives. I don't know of anyone who gets out of life without suffering physical afflictions. Those who suffer most teach us best. "God gave me this illness to remind me that I'm not number One; he is" (Muhammad Ali).

"The Son of Man hath descended below them all. Art thou greater than he? (D&C 122:8).

A Testimony Can Get Us Through Anything

Life will cast all of us into our share of fiery furnaces. We don't have much say about how we enter, but how we exit will depend on what we do while we're going through. To make it to the Promised Land, we've got to keep moving forward, even if we have to limp the entire way.

> John R. Moyle lived in Alpine, Utah, about 22 miles as the crow flies to the Salt Lake Temple, where he was the chief superintendent of masonry during its construction. To make certain he was always at work by 8 o'clock, Brother Moyle would start walking about 2 A.M. on Monday mornings. He would finish his work week at 5 P.M. on Friday and then start the walk home, arriving there shortly before midnight. Each week he would repeat that schedule for the entire time he served on the construction of the temple.
>
> Once when he was home on the weekend, one of his cows bolted during milking and kicked Brother Moyle in the leg, shattering the bone just below the knee. With no better medical help than they had in such rural circumstances, his family and friends took a door off the hinges and strapped him onto that makeshift operating table. They then took the bucksaw they had been using to cut branches from a nearby tree and amputated his leg just a few inches below the knee. When against all medical likelihood the leg finally started to heal, Brother Moyle took a piece of wood and carved an artificial leg. First he walked in the house. Then he walked around the yard. Finally he ventured out about his property. When he felt he could stand the pain, he strapped on his leg, walked the 22 miles to the Salt Lake Temple, climbed the scaffolding, and with a chisel in his hand hammered out the declaration "Holiness to the Lord" (Jeffrey R. Holland, "As Doves to Our Windows," *Ensign,* May 2000, 76).

We might lack the strength or the sense of direction to make it out of our trials on the Promised Land side, but the Lord's strength is sufficient. His sense of direction is truer than true north. I have come to know personally that life is about getting "through" one thing after another, and learning to enjoy each experience, each moment. It's all about making progress only the Lord can measure. "Ye cannot behold with your natural eyes, for the present time, the design of your God concerning those things which shall . . . follow after much tribulation. For after much tribulation come the blessings" (D&C 58:3–4).

THE LORD WAITS ON US

Number five is a reminder that when we come through our fiery furnaces, the Savior awaits us. He cheers us, He anticipates us, He believes in us, even when our faith in ourselves wavers. Most of the time God works from behind the scenes, from the other side—wherever that may be.

Whether our steps of faith be baby steps or giant leaps, they will be met with opposition. Once we start to go through our trials, Satan will attempt to trip us. He wants us to fall and to stay down. He wants us to believe that the terrain is too treacherous, the curves too sharp, the path to perfection unattainable. He wants to waylay us, to delay us, and to get us lost entirely. One of the ways he does that is to tell us we walk the road alone. That's a big fat lie to make us feel frustrated and to get us to fail. I recall a meeting where a minister asked the massive audience, "If you came here to save yourself, please raise your hands."

Tens of thousands of hands shot in the air.

"Too bad," she said, smiling. "None of us can save ourselves. Only God can do that for us."

Jesus Christ walked "*through* the valley of the shadow of death." (Ps. 23:4).

He took no shortcuts. No easy detours. And He did not let the adversary delay Him in His work. He went through life until He could say, "It is finished" (John 19:30).

Only then was He able to ascend to His Father who awaited His glorious homecoming.

The Answer Is in the Atonement

The questions that appear to have no answers can find resolution in the power of the Atonement. Do you recall when Jesus taught some difficult doctrine and was virtually abandoned by all but his twelve Apostles?

We do not know the heaviness of His heart as he asked, "Will ye also go away?" And Peter said, "Lord, to whom shall we go? thou hast the words of eternal life. And we believe and are sure that thou art that Christ, the Son of the living God" (John 6:67–69).

It does not matter where you hurt. Jesus can heal you.

It does not matter how far you have wandered. Jesus can bring you home.

It does not matter who you are. He knows your heart.

"The Son of God suffereth according to the flesh that he might take upon him the sins of his people, that he might blot out their transgressions according to the power of his deliverance; and now behold, this is the testimony which is in me" (Alma 7:13).

The testimony that is within me sings, "I know that my Redeemer lives." He lives and leads the way. Any darkness that we may encounter is nothing compared to the blackness that engulfed Jesus as He knelt in the Garden of Gethsemane. Any betrayal that wounds us cannot compete with the kiss of Judas. The loneliness we suffer cannot compare with Christ's feelings of being forsaken as He submitted His perfect life to the will of His Father. Our cries are only whimpers compared to the agony the Savior suffered at the apparent withdrawal of the Father's Spirit, which "evoked the greatest soul cry in human history" (James E. Talmage, *Jesus the Christ,* 613).

We are no ordinary people. We are chosen to stand tall, remain steady, and stay the course, no matter what comes. Shadrach, Meshach, and Abed-nego did it. Abinadi did it. Joseph and Hyrum Smith did it. Our prophet today is a prime example of someone willing to "go through" any trial necessary to get to the other side where the Lord waits with open arms.

I only half joke when I say after our tribulation comes our trial. It is a time to ask, "Master, carest thou not that [I] perish?" (Mark 4:38).

He cares.

He knows our struggles.

He knows our strengths.

He has given the scriptures to us, and no matter what trial we face, we can discover how to deal with it somewhere between the book of Genesis and the book of Moses.

Shadrach, Meshach, and Abed-nego were saved from a fiery death.

So was Abinadi. Even though his body burned, he made it through and we can too, because Jesus Christ is on the other side waiting.

This I know.

This I promise.

CHAPTER SEVEN

It's Who You Know

Behold, I stand at the door, and knock;
if any man hear my voice,
and open the door, I will come in to him,
and will sup with him, and he with me.
—*Revelation 3:20*

I met Barbara on a river-rafting trip. She is a wealthy, influential, and well-connected business woman who has traveled the world many times. She has been educated in the finest schools, and she is conversant in four languages. Barbara has met U.S. presidents and dined with world leaders.

While we were looking up at the nighttime stars and the boundless wonder of God's Rocky Mountain creations, I spoke in reverential tones of my awe. "Wow!" was the most profound expression I could muster.

She brushed the dust off her hands and scoffed at me. "You don't really believe there's a god up there sitting on a cloud watching us, do you?"

"I don't believe He's sitting on a cloud," I said.

Barbara was appalled. "You must be desperate to have to cling to such nonsense."

"Are you an atheist?" I asked.

"No. I'm not saying there is no god; I just don't believe there is."

Remember Korihor? He said something hauntingly similar: "I do not deny the existence of a God, but I do not believe that there is a God" (Alma 30:48).

Barbara is no Korihor, just a woman navigating her way without faith. Over time we became friends, and one day there was a shift in the way she posed her query, "Do you really *know* God?"

"Yes," I said.

Talk about manna to the soul!

"I know some people in high places," she joked, "but not *that* high."

My heart burned and my throat swelled like I'd swallowed an orange. Tears trickled down my cheeks. I could not stop my hands from trembling. Barbara no doubt thought I was a basket case, but I knew that the Holy Ghost was doing what the Holy Ghost does—he was teaching and testifying to me.

Me, little old, insignificant me—a woman ordinary as oatmeal—knew in that moment that I was as blessed as any woman could be. Without wealth or prestige, I had connections that rose to the highest, holiest place. I had the address to heaven, the phone number, and a security code allowing me access at any time I needed help.

We all have that same invaluable data; the information is embedded in our spirits. We are daughters of Deity. "Ask, and it shall be given you; seek, and ye shall find; knock, and it shall be opened unto you. For every one that asketh receiveth" (Luke 11:9–10). The scripture does not say only perfect women who sew flawlessly will receive. It does not say only women who are size six, with no dust bunnies lurking behind their refrigerators, will have their prayers answered.

News flash. *All* of us are imperfect women loved with a perfect, unfaltering love. Knowing that is the sweetest and also the most savory manna there is.

Every mother matters.

Every child counts.

Our divine link is direct and our access limited only by our worthiness and desire to establish a personal relationship with heaven. I assure you that you will never make that attempt, only to hear the phone ring and ring, with no one at home on the other end to answer. You call. He'll answer. I give you my solemn promise.

While I was still in college I was employed as a writer with the entertainment industry. It was my job to interview artists, write articles, and assist with public relations. I quickly learned what is meant by, "It's who you know." If I knew the right people, spoke the right names, doors would open. If not, doors would remain closed.

So it is with Heaven. If we want access to the Father there is only one name that is the key. "There shall be no other name given nor any other way nor means whereby salvation can come unto the children of men, only in and through the name of Christ" (Mosiah 3:17).

The book of Revelation contains a standing invitation. "Behold, I stand at the door, and knock: if any man hear my voice, and open the door, I will come in to him, and will sup with him, and he with me" (Rev. 3:20). Imagine dining on manna with the Master.

If we expect a better invitation, it's not going to come.

I've already confessed that I continually hunger for help in raising my children. How do I keep them on the straight and narrow? What do I do if they stray? How do I love them like they deserve?

I counted 84 books on parenting tips the other day at the bookstore. Authors who are experts with all of the answers, right? Nope. Only one Author has the answers because He is the supreme Parent. He knows us and He knows our children. If we know Him, we can know what to do and have the strength to do it.

For some time following the experience with my friend Barbara, I was mistaken in thinking that because I knew that God was the Father and Jesus the Son, I knew them. Let me repeat. I was mistaken in thinking that because I knew that God was the Father and Jesus the Son, I knew them.

There is a difference between knowing who someone is and *knowing* that person. An introduction is not a relationship. I desired a *relationship* with my Heavenly Father and Savior Jesus Christ. I wanted to hear and recognize the promptings of the Holy Spirit. Jesus taught the Nephites that, "the Father, and the Son, and the Holy Ghost are one" (3 Ne. 11:27).

Joseph Smith explained how to obtain a working, loving relationship with heaven. "After any portion of the human family are made acquainted with the important fact that there is a God, who has created and does uphold all things, the extent of their knowledge respecting his character and glory will depend upon their diligence and faithfulness in seeking after him . . ." (*Lectures on Faith,* 2:55).

To know Jesus Christ like I desired, to establish the kind of relationship that my soul hungered for, meant I had to be diligent and faithful in seeking after Him. Brigham Young taught that it was not an introduction I sought, but a reintroduction. "You are well acquainted with God our Heavenly Father, or the great Elohim. You are all well acquainted with Him for there is not a soul of you but what has lived in His house and dwelt with Him year after year, and yet you are seeking to become acquainted with Him, when the fact is, you have merely forgotten what you did know" (*Journal of Discourses* 4:216).

When you are made acquainted with someone and want to know them better, what do you do? You spend time together. My children "hang out" with their friends to get better acquainted. I decided to "hang out" with Jesus. I'm not being flip or disrespectful, but I knew I would have to make an investment of my time to get the results I desired. So I made a commitment to pray more often and more fervently. I took President Hinckley's advice to heart. "We need to meditate, contemplate, think about what we are praying about and for, and then speak to the Lord as one person speaks to another" (*Standing for Something*, 2000, 116).

After years of rushing through my prayers, repeating the same apologies and requests, I became a little self-conscious about my new approach. Satan whispered that I wasn't worthy to pray so sincerely, and who did I think I was to expect God to answer my pleas? I was a sinner, a woman who said and did things out of harmony with heaven. That's how the devil works. Anytime we attempt to do right, he attempts to block us. Brigham Young pegged that strategy decades ago. "If the Devil says you cannot pray when you are angry, tell him it is none of his business, and pray until that species of insanity is dispelled and serenity is restored to the mind" (*Discourses of Brigham Young*, 10:175).

I prayed with a new approach and a new voice. Talking *about* God was different than talking to Him, or ultimately, with Him. At first, I felt like a little child, struggling and stumbling over my own words. It made me think of a story Charles B. Vaughn told of a grandfather walking with his granddaughter when he heard her repeating the alphabet in a prayer-like tone.

"What are you doing, honey?" he asked.

"I'm praying," said the girl, "but I can't think of exactly the right words, so I'm just saying all the letters. God will put them together for me, because He knows what I'm thinking."

That little girl was right. God knows what is in our hearts and minds.

We are all acquainted with people who monopolize the conversation. They talk. We listen. They talk. We nod. They talk. We nod off.

And so, contrary to my verbose nature, I learned to divide my prayer time fifty-fifty. Real generous of me, don't you think? Ten minutes for my speech and ten minutes for me to be still and allow for rebuttal. That is not what the Lord meant when He said, "Be still and know that I am God" (D&C 101:16).

My fifty-fifty pattern of prayer did not work. I knew heaven was available to me, but I could not offer the prayer of a Pharisee and expect the miracles due a Saint. So I took to heart the Lord's admonition to "pray always." I prayed about everything that mattered and I prayed everywhere I went. I learned that prayer is a machine with two basic parts: asking and receiving. Gratitude greases the gears and keeps it working. Now I tell my children, "Thank the Lord for a lot and ask him for a little." I tell them that because I've tested it; it works.

So began a journey that continues to this moment. Prayer upon prayer, I learned to pray. I tried to keep my mind and heart as open as my mouth. I listened, and I learned the infinite power behind a sincere petition, and that effective prayer has nothing at all to do with the words, the length, or the poetry, but everything to do with the purpose and the faith of the petitioner.

The first prayer I ever offered as a child was, "God is great, God is good, let us thank Him for our food." I have no doubt that the simplest prayers, when uttered sincerely, reach the highest heavens. Just as I have no doubt that the most eloquent prayers, offered in length and in light of those we would have see and admire us for our awesome spirituality, float upward with the levity of a bowling ball.

God does not care where we pray, how we pray. He only cares that we pray with sincerity.

"Prayer is the way and means, given us by our Creator, whereby we can counsel and communicate with him," taught Elder Bruce R. McConkie. "It is one of the chief cornerstones of pure and perfect worship" ("Patterns of Prayer," *Ensign*, May 1984, 32).

Sincere prayer takes practice, but the power is real. It is no fluke that the divine command to pray is repeated more often than any other mandate.

Brigham Young advised that for prayer to be effectual,

> it is often difficult and strenuous—just plain hard work. If you really want to converse with the Lord, you must count on a mighty struggle. Receiving inspiration and revelation through

> prayer is one of the greatest achievements of man, and to expect that blessing without effort is contrary to the order of heaven. One has to break the prayer barrier by knocking and knocking. We should not be dismayed when much knocking at first seems to avail little. There are few exercises in faith greater than praying persistently, and the very act of knocking will capacitate us to accept, understand, and implement the newfound truths that may be revealed to us. Nothing teaches us to pray more effectively than forcing ourselves to pray. However, as in skiing, the "learning how" can be exciting—the realization that we are participating in an effort that has brought most, if not all, celestial truths to the earth creates a sense of spiritual adventure second to none (*Journal of Discourses,* 12:155).

I challenge you to fall on your knees and let the adventure begin!

Next, in my ongoing quest to know the Lord, I began a serious study of His character. The prophet Joseph Smith stated, "It is the first principle of the gospel to know for a certainty the character of God, and to know that we may converse with Him as one man converses with another (*Teachings of the Prophet Joseph Smith*, 345).

One of the first things I came to realize is that there is true and living power in the very name of Jesus Christ. Paul explained to the Philippians: "Wherefore God also hath highly exalted him, and given him a name which is above every name. That at the name of Jesus every knee should bow, of things in heaven, and things in earth, and things under the earth; And that every tongue should confess that Jesus Christ is Lord, to the glory of God the Father" (Philip. 2:9–11).

Never again would my Savior's high and holy name be a mere tag at the end of my prayers.

I already knew that the Lord stands ready to hear and answer our petitions, to feed us the manna for which we hunger, but now I was ready to find out all I could about what He is really like.

The other night I overheard my teenage daughter say to her friend, "Tell me about so-and-so. He asked me out, and before I say yes, I want to find out about him."

My approach was much the same. I wanted to find out about the Lord so I went to those who were already acquainted with Him. I did that through continued prayer and personal revelation, also by delving into the scriptures, and studying the words of the prophets.

I made a list of attributes and observations. Jesus Christ is the Firstborn, the Son of the Eternal Father, in both spirit and flesh. He was once as we are now.

We dwelt with Him before the foundations of this world were laid. He is the Creator who "made heaven, and earth, and the sea, and the fountains of water" (Rev. 14:7). He is the one who stepped forward and said, "Father, thy will be done, and the glory be thine forever" (Moses 4:2). He came to this earth, born of an earthly mother, to save us from our sins. He is our advocate, the intercessory for us. Christ is the light, the life, the truth. He dwelt in a personal tabernacle, having a body of flesh and bones. He is all knowing and all powerful. Unchanging. No one will ever ascend above Him or replace Him. He lived upon this earth as the great Exemplar, He suffered all things, and has empathy for us no matter our condition. While here, Christ set up His Church, called Apostles to carry on His word, ordained and set apart select ones to carry forth His work. He blessed them. He has a tenderness and devotion to children. His mission was to save souls. He did the will of His father and lived a flawless life. Innocent and perfect at the age of 33, vile, murderous hands betrayed Him; friends betrayed Him. They spit upon Him, mocked Him, humiliated Him, lied about Him, and Jesus Christ lifted His eyes and prayed, "Father forgive them" (Luke 23:34). He was lifted upon the cross by His enemies and crucified. He atoned for our sins because He loves us with an unconditional love. He paved the way and made it possible for us to return to our Father's presence to enjoy eternal life, and He did this out of a love that knows no bounds and stretches throughout all eternity.

He is the lawgiver and is obedient to His own laws. His patience is infinite and His mercy made new every morning. When we sincerely repent, He will forgive our trespasses. Though we are faithless, Jesus Christ is always faithful, and He will never fail us.

His mission was a complete success and now he lives as an exalted man in heaven—a resurrected, glorified person. His ultimate desire is to have us become like Him, to share with us all the Father has given Him. Jesus Christ, in all His power and glory, knows His children. He answers prayers. He answered the prayer of a faithful fourteen-year-old boy named Joseph Smith.

Through the whisperings and wonderment of the Holy Spirit, I came to know for myself, not just the facts, but the fact that Jesus Christ knows you; He knows me. He loves us. His love is perfect even though we are not. Elder Neal A. Maxwell reminds us that "A universal God is actually involved with our small, individual universes of experience! In the midst of His vast dominions, yet He numbers us, knows us, and loves us perfectly"("Yet Thou Art There," *Ensign*, Nov. 1987, 30).

These are but a few of the character traits and attributes of the Savior. Make your own list. Study it. Ponder it. Come to know for yourself the provider of all manna.

Thirdly, I attempted to emulate the Savior. "Come follow me . . ." said the Savior. I accepted that invitation.

Albert Schweitzer said, "Example is not the main thing in influencing others—it is the only thing."

Elder Bruce R. McConkie explained, "To become like him, we have to have the same character, perfections, and attributes that he possesses" (*Words for Women*, 98).

What an undertaking! But so true. If we want what someone has, we have to do what they did to get it. The Savior was obedient; I'm a bit of a rebel. The Savior was loving; I reserve my affection. The Savior's mood was constant; mine fluctuates like the wind.

It mattered not that my effort was pitiful. What mattered is the effort I put forth. How many times have you comforted a fallen child with the tender words, "You tried and that's all that really matters." Heavenly Father always rewards effort.

I enjoy rock climbing. Only fools climb alone with no one at the other end of the rope to assist, encourage, or catch them if they fall. I think of Jesus Christ as the One at the end of our ropes belaying us, encouraging our every effort. When we slip—and we all do—He holds the rope, takes up the slack, and with His unfailing strength and supreme stamina, keeps us from hitting the ground. Then it's back up we go, higher than we were before.

Once when I was upset with one of my children—and let's not pretend—I was out of sync with the Spirit. I said things like, "If I've told you once, I've told you a thousand times . . . As long as you live under my roof . . . You're out of chances with me!"

Somewhere in that tirade the Spirit was able to break through to me. Before me was set out the example of the Savior, the kind of parent He is to me. Never once has He said, "If I've told you once, I've told you a thousand times . . . As long as you live under my roof! (now that's what I call high ceilings) . . . You're out of chances with me!" Never once—though I've given Him reason countless times.

Our Father parents with rules that have consequences. He allows us to suffer those consequences, just as He showers us with blessings when we are obedient.

When we fall short He does not condemn us. He does not limit our chances. How foolish, then, was I as a mother to think I had the right to do the same to my child?

The next time I asked my daughter, "Have you cleaned your room?" when obviously she hadn't, I stopped my natural tongue and said simply, "Then clean it."

The experience was manna to both of us.

As a primary teacher I learned that motto, "What would Jesus do?" We don't always know, but we can know if we are open to inspiration and continually seek to know. It's like an ongoing lesson in parenting and the teacher is always available, if we do not let our feelings or our emotions chase it away. "The Spirit does not get our attention by shouting or shaking us with a heavy hand. Rather it whispers. It caresses so gently that if we are preoccupied we may not feel it at all. These delicate, refined spiritual communications are not seen with our eyes, nor heard with our ears. And even though it is described as a voice, it is a voice that one feels, more than one hears" (Boyd K. Packer, "The Candle of the Lord," *Ensign*, Jan. 1983, 52–53).

My journey to become like Jesus is just underway. I'm still at the bottom of the mountain, but as I continue to remember Him and follow Him I find fresh insight in Nephi's counsel to us to "feast upon the words of Christ; for behold, the words of Christ will tell you all things what ye should do" (2 Ne. 32:3). There is no better handbook for parents than the Book of Mormon. And no better guide than the Holy Spirit. The Spirit's mellowing, softening influence can fill us with "love, joy, peace, longsuffering, gentleness, goodness, faith" (Gal. 5:22).

What manna!

The final step in following the Savior is to do as He did. He served others. It is never enough just to do the right thing; our hearts have to be pure. We must do the right thing for the right reason.

Have you ever baked a casserole or taught a lesson just to fulfill an assignment? "I don't know why I'm doing this. I have such a lousy attitude, I won't get any blessings. They'll just eat my casserole and never bring my dish back. No one will care that I spent ten hours preparing this lesson. What does it matter?"

It matters.

If you can't serve with an attitude of love, serve anyway. Keep serving until you learn to love the people you serve. Mop the floor because you love those little feet that will tromp over it. Make the meal because those you love are hungry. Serve because you love. On a personal note, I feel miserable and used and exhausted when I serve with my mind focused on the service I am rendering. But . . . when I shift my focus to the people I am serving, and why I am serving them, when I remember who serves me, then I feel rejuvenated by my efforts. It's like exercise for the spirit. Nephi taught the same principle with the power of a prophet: "Ye must not perform any thing unto the Lord save in the first place ye shall pray unto the Father in the name of Christ, that he will consecrate thy performance unto thee, that thy performance may be for the welfare of thy soul" (2 Ne. 32:9).

It's who you know. Know the people you serve. They are no different from the people that Jesus served. We are one eternal family.

Keep this assurance in mind as you attempt to emulate the divine. "God our Father, Jesus, our Elder Brother and our Redeemer, and the Holy Ghost, the Testator, are perfect. They know us best and love us most and will not leave one thing undone for our eternal welfare" (Ezra Taft Benson, "The Great Commandment—Love the Lord," *Ensign*, May 1988, 5).

"Just do the best you can each day. Do the basic things and, before you realize it, your life will be full of spiritual understanding that will confirm to you that your Heavenly Father loves you. When a person knows this, then life will be full of purpose and meaning" (M. Russell Ballard, "Keeping Life's Demands In Balance," *Ensign*, May 1987, 16).

"There is something grand in the consideration of the fact that the Lord loves us with a most ardent love. The love that a woman exercises toward her offspring cannot equal the love that God exercises toward us. He never leaves us. He is always before us, and upon our right hand and our left hand. Continually He watches over us" (Lorenzo Snow, *CR*, Oct. 1898, 2).

It's who you know.

My friend Barbara has never joined the Church.

Not long ago she asked again, "Do you truly believe you know God?"

"I'm beginning to," I told her, and my soul smiled.

The seventh chapter of the book of Matthew sums up the quest we undertake to know the Savior. In His own words: "Wherefore by their fruits ye shall know them. Not every one that saith unto me, Lord, Lord, shall enter into the kingdom of heaven; but he that doeth the will of my Father which is in heaven. Many will say to me in that day, Lord, Lord, have we not prophesied in thy name? and in thy name have cast out devils? and in thy name done many wonderful works? And then will I profess unto them, I never knew you: depart from me, ye that work iniquity. Therefore whosoever heareth these sayings of mine, and doeth them, I will liken him unto a wise man, which built his house upon a rock: And the rain descended, and the floods came, and the winds blew, and beat upon that house; and it fell not: for it was founded upon a rock" (Matt. 7:20–25).

Sisters, let our rock, our foundation, be Jesus Christ. Let us climb up higher to where our vantage point is clearer.

Let us dedicate our lives to knowing Him, to trusting that if we lose our grip, He will not let us tumble to the bottom. Let us understand that Christ atoned for our sins, and let us also understand *why* He would make such a supreme sacrifice. To become a true disciple of Jesus Christ, we must know for ourselves that He is the Son of God. That sure testimony comes only through the Holy Ghost, who shall "shall teach you all things, and bring all things to your remembrance" (John 14:26).

Remember. Remember what Brigham Young said. "You know much about him, if you did but realize it" (*Journal of Discourses*, 8:30).

Let us study and search His words for the manna that our hungry souls seek. Let us write down and record every answered prayer, every inspiration and instruction that He gives us. Let our book of remembrance be complete. "The good word of God with which we must nourish is the simple doctrine of the gospel" (Henry B. Eyring, "Feed My Lambs," *Ensign*, Nov. 1997, 84).

Let our fruits be the fruit of love. Sweet, ripe manna for all we encounter.

Let us love Him who first loved us. "If ye love me, keep my commandments," said Jesus. We do not keep the commandments to earn His love. That's not how it works. We are already recipients of that perfect love. We just have to be willing to receive it. He loves us and if we love Him, we will love others. We will serve them out of love. I have come to know for myself that God doesn't care nearly as much about *what* we do as *why* we do it. Let our motive always be love.

As we climb higher, as we trust the One who holds our rope, let us search for His face in the faces of those whom we serve. And when finally, we come face to face with our Savior, may we recognize His voice and hear those words we long to hear, "Come unto me, for I know you; you are the one who kept climbing and trusted that I would not let you fall."

CHAPTER EIGHT

Halfway Home

Feast upon the words of Christ, for behold,
the words of Christ will tell you all things what ye should do.
——2 Nephi 32:3

I was newly married, newly sprung from college drudgery, I had my first real job and first real paycheck. I decided to go crazy and splurge.

I bought a coat. My first nice winter coat. It was kitten gray and just that soft. It was the only coat I had ever owned that fell clear to my ankles to keep out the bitter winter wind. It had big, black buttons and deep, satiny pockets with no holes. I wrapped myself in it and fell in love all over again.

I know it sounds crazy to fall in love with a coat, but that's what happened. I bought the coat in December and by January we were cherished pals. Inseparable. Until one day when I was driving home from work. Of course I was wearing my coat; there were three-foot snow drifts along the streets, icy slush, and a vicious north wind.

I was happy. I was warm. I was blessed.

Then I saw her. She was walking along the sidewalk. She couldn't have been much older than me—early twenties. Thin with long, dark hair and no coat at all. Just a wispy dress that blew against her like those pictures you see of the Little Match Box Girl. I shivered.

The traffic light changed and my car rolled to a stop within a few feet of the woman. I could see how cold and miserable she was.

"Give your coat to her," a voice said.

I turned off the radio and looked around. I was the only one in my car and the windows were rolled up tight.

"Hurry. Take your coat off and give it to the woman."

I recognized the voice. It was the Spirit of the Holy Ghost.

"Don't tell me what to do," I said aloud.

"Hurry," said the Spirit. "Give her your coat."

"But the coat is new," I whined. "It's nice and it's mine."

"Hurry," the Spirit said again.

The woman walked past. The traffic light turned green. A car behind me honked. I drove off in my warm car, wrapped snugly in my warm coat. I got all the way to the end of the block before I started to suffocate in that coat. I turned around and went back to give the woman my coat. It was a long, straight street with an endless sidewalk.

Fat, flaky snow was beginning to cover my windshield. I turned on my wipers and slowed down to locate the woman. She had vanished. I spent the next hour driving up and down that street, up and down, praying that she would emerge so that I could do what I should have done.

I even parked my car and knocked on doors in the area. No one knew who I described. And by this time the Holy Ghost had gone silent.

I went home, soaked and smelling like a wet cat. I rehearsed my blunder to my husband. "What if she was one of the Three Nephites and I failed to help her?" I sobbed.

He rolled his eyes and handed me a tissue. "The Three Nephites aren't women."

I went to the closet and hung up my coat. The kitteny fabric was starting to itch me anyway. Sometime during the night when it had dried, I wrapped it in a plastic cover and shut the door so I didn't have to look at it.

The next day I took that coat, still wrapped in plastic, back to that street and waited. No sign of the woman. I went back again and again. I tried to find her all the way into April.

I felt guilty.

I felt sorry.

I felt stupid.

I couldn't wear the coat because I had been told to give it away. Out of selfishness, I'd kept it and what was once a blessing was now a burden.

Sometime later our doorbell rang. There stood a beautiful woman, thin, with long, dark hair. I knew it wasn't the woman from winter, but the entire episode was suddenly before me.

"I babysit," the woman said. "Do you need anyone to babysit your children?"

We had no children yet but I scrutinized the woman. She didn't look like a Nephite, so I probably wasn't being tested again. I stood there waiting for the Spirit tell me what to do. It said nothing.

"Wait here, please," I said, darting down the hallway to the closet. I came back and shoved the plastic-covered, long, gray coat at the woman. "Here, take this please."

She stared at me a little like my husband had. "I'm not cold," she said. "It's July."

"Yes, I know. I know. I want you to have the coat though. It's a gift."

I hurried and shut the door before she could decline my offer.

When the Spirit speaks to us—and we have no doubt that it is the Spirit of the Lord—we had better listen. We had better obey. To this day, I wonder what would have happened if I had given that first woman my coat. I will never know.

Giving it away to the second woman did not assuage my guilt or make me obedient. It did get rid of the coat though, and I was glad for that. It was beginning to meow at me every time I opened the closet.

As Latter-day Saint women, ours is the responsibility to emulate Jesus Christ. To follow His teachings, the paths He trod. In short, to love as He loved.

While it's not easy, it is not as difficult as we often make it.

"The completed beauty of Christ's life is only the added beauty of little inconspicuous acts of beauty—talking with the woman at the well; showing the young ruler the stealthy ambition laid away in his heart that kept him out of the Kingdom of Heaven; . . . teaching a little knot of followers how to pray; kindling a fire and broiling fish that his disciples might have a breakfast waiting for them when they came ashore from a night of fishing, cold, tired, and discouraged. All of these things, you see, let us in so easily into the real quality and tone of [Christ's] interests, so specific, so narrowed down, so enlisted in what is small, so engrossed with what is minute" (Charles Henry Parkhurst, "Kindness and Love," in *Leaves of Gold,* 177).

Our little acts of kindness make a big difference in the quality of our lives. I have taught my children to ask themselves "What would Jesus do?"

One day my son, in a bath of tears, looked up at me and said, "I don't know, Mom. I don't know what Jesus would do. I'm not Jesus. I'm just a kid."

All of us are just "kids"—some of us more childish than childlike. We feel inferior. Inadequate. Incompetent. It's time for us to get over those feelings. They only get in the way. They distract us from doing good, which is what the scriptures tell us Jesus did, day in and day out. None of us will ever face the trials Christ did, but we have His example to follow, and as long as we are willing, He will lead us home.

As long as we are willing. Willing to follow the Spirit. Willing to keep His commandments. In three words: Willing to love, love, love.

A Willing Spirit

My husband was called to a leadership position and asked what his most important responsibility was. "Just show up. You can't imagine," said our bishop, "how many people make promises and never show up to keep them."

We all know what it means when the spirit is willing but the flesh is weak. We want to get out of bed early to help Sister Jones move. To weed the flowerbed at the church. To scrub the garbage pails in the ward nursery.

In this Church, every member matters. If we don't show up, someone else has to carry out our responsibilities or they don't get carried out. The Divine design is counter to the world's design: we do need each other. We are codependent on each other and on our Father. We are a family. It is our duty to serve and to love each other.

How? That is the question. "The truest help we can render an afflicted man is not to take his burden from him, but to call out his best energy, that he may be able to bear the burden" (Phillips Brooks).

Lifting those burdens sometimes means lifting excuses out of the way. Too many times we make excuses for why we can't serve. Most of them are selfish, like mine. Thomas S. Monson relates another coat story with an entirely different ending. Joseph Smith approached John E. Page and announced, "Brother Page, you have been called on a mission to Canada."

I have no doubt that Brother Page's spirit was willing; it was his flesh that shivered. Canada was cold. "Brother Joseph, I can't go to Canada. I don't have a coat to wear."

The Prophet did not hesitate. He took off his own coat and handed it to John Page. "Wear this," he said, "and the Lord will bless you."

Two years later John Page had walked some 5,000 miles and baptized 600 converts into the Lord's fold ("How Do We Show Our Love?" *Ensign,* Jan. 1998, 2).

What is our responsibility as members of that same fold? To fight the flesh and "love one another" (John 13:34).

A Willing Mind

Inspiration comes to those who strive to be worthy and open to the Spirit's whisperings. Dale Clark is an elderly man who lives in northern Utah. He is a member of The Church of Jesus Christ of Latter-day Saints. When he was young his mind was open to the inspiration that young people could make a difference in Third World countries. His spirit was willing, his mind was willing, and then Brother Clark set out to prove "his whole heart and soul" were willing. The result was the International Volunteer Service, which he said later evolved into the Peace Corps.

None of us knows the ideas and inspiration that can come to us if our minds are open to the promptings of the Spirit.

When we see a person in need we often don't know what to do. We fear doing the wrong thing. We fear offending someone. We fear our effort will be rejected. So what? If we don't move forward, who will? "God does notice us, and he watches over us. But it is usually through another person that he meets our needs. Therefore, it is vital that we serve each other in the kingdom" (Spencer W. Kimball, "Small Acts of Service," *Ensign*, Dec. 1974, 5).

Let us be the one willing to take the risk and make the effort to be that person the Lord can count on.

In the same breath, remember that genuine service requires all of our resources: our time, our energy, our thoughts, sometimes our finances. We can empty ourselves if all we do is give and never receive.

A Willing Mouth

Having a willing mouth was no problem for me—until I realized that our mouths have to be willing to remain shut when they have oh, so much to say. Elder Henry Eyring teaches "There are two great keys to inviting the Spirit to guide what words we speak as we feed others. They are the daily study of the scriptures and the prayer of faith" ("Feed My Lambs," *Ensign,* Nov. 1997, 83).

A daily study of the scriptures isn't so we can quote a chapter and verse as much as it is to make us open to what the Lord would have us say. "My spirit, even the comforter, . . . shall give him, in the very hour, what he shall say" (D&C 124:97).

Nephi teaches us that we should pray for those whom we serve. There is no leading if there is no loving. "For I pray continually for [my people] by day, and mine eyes water my pillow by night, because of them" (2 Ne. 33:3).

Two of the places where I am reaping benefits from being willing to keep my mouth closed are at home and at church.

Church? It's the place we should be able to go to renew our spiritual strength, to partake of the sacrament and renew our covenants, to fellowship and edify. It should be a safe harbor where we should never feel judged or *mis*judged. "Attending Church is, or should be, a respite from the pressures of everyday life. It should bring peace and contentment" (Boyd K. Packer, "Parents In Zion," *Ensign*, Nov. 1998, 23).

The words that come out of our mouths at church should always we weighted with love and true inspiration. Love, as always, is the motivator.

The second place a closed mouth can be a blessing is at home. I learned this during a time in our family when contention was not the exception, but the rule. Bickering and quarreling chased the Spirit of the Lord right out the door. I thought everyone else was guilty. I never suspected myself. So I got down on my knees and prayed that I would be willing to do whatever it took to reform those guilty.

The next morning I awoke with a wretched case of laryngitis.

I couldn't speak for nearly a week. Know what? It was a time of revelation for me. I learned it wasn't just what I said; it was how I said it. "Practice the piano." "Clean your room." I learned that when I couldn't talk *back*, or use that certain tone of voice, my children were more willing to talk to me.

A willing mouth isn't always an open mouth.

A Willing Hand

When we work together to benefit those in need, "we eliminate the weakness of one person standing alone and substitute the strength of many serving together. While we may not be able to do everything, we can and must do something" (Thomas S. Monson, "Our Brothers' Keepers," *Ensign,* June. 1998, 39).

Georgia Rassmussen is a visiting teacher who exemplifies this principle. She may just be the best visiting teacher ever. I know because for ten years she served me. She served quietly, faithfully, and willingly, and I'm not easy to serve. I cherish my independence.

We can't always be totally independent. One of those times came during the ninth month of pregnancy. It was the middle of the night when I felt the first contraction. Then the second. "Can't you wait till morning?" my sleepy husband asked.

Another contraction. "Nope." And I called Georgia to come quickly and stay with our young daughters while my husband drove me to the hospital to be checked.

"The baby's not due for weeks, so I'm sure it's a false alarm. I'll probably be back in an hour."

Two days later I gave birth to our son Collin.

I never worried about our girls. Georgia stayed with them until my aunt could come, and I knew they were safe. How can you thank someone for providing that kind of security?

Georgia learned such Christlike charity from her own family history. One of her progenitors, John Kenney, was an early convert to the gospel. He lived in the Utah territory during the final days of polygamy and married two wives, both on the same day. Imagine if you will, the feelings those women held for one another.

Not what you might suspect. There was no jealousy or animosity between them. That is evidenced in the fact that they each named their firstborn daughters after the other.

The Kenney family resided in a small southern Utah town. The two wives lived in separate modest houses on either side of town.

One morning John Kenney, loaded with cargo, turned his wagon toward Nevada. He never returned.

The women remained in that small town, they remained loyal to each other, the best of friends. The truest of sisters. When one had quilting to do, the other was there to assist. On the days bread was to be baked, the women baked together. On the days devoted to washing, the women shared each other's company as well as laundry.

Their example of love and devotion to each other touched the small town. The people would see these two women, when chores were done at the end of the day, always, always walk each other halfway home.

Can we, Sisters, take one less step than they did? Not when the Lord has asked that we bring each and every one of his children all the way back home.

A WILLING HEART

We women are blessed with willing hearts. Open hearts.

A mother is any woman who cares for and cares about God's children.

A willing heart is a scarred heart because it gets broken, only to be healed by the Master Physician's touch.

Church history teaches us a perfect example of a willing heart. During his last days at Carthage, the Prophet Joseph was surrounded by his brother Hyrum, Willard Richards, and John Taylor. Love for the Lord and love for each other bound them together as their lives hung in the balance.

Brother Richards looked into the blue eyes of the Prophet and he said, "Joseph, if you are condemned to die, I will die in your place."

Joseph was the prophet and knew that was not possible. "But Willard," he said, "you cannot do that."

"Yes, Joseph," Brother Richards replied, "but I will" (see *History of the Church*, 6:616).

A willing heart is willing to love. It is willing to forgive. It is willing to live and die for what it knows to be true. Jesus is the reason it beats.

The Lord knows our hearts. He knows our minds and our works. He loves us for all that we do. He has sent a prophet to direct us, leaders to love us, words to strengthen us.

Service isn't something that can always be tracked and graded. We don't always know how we are performing. That cannot stop us from doing what we feel directed to do. From serving with love.

From the great mind and heart of Albert Schweitzer: "Not one of us knows what effect his life produces, and what he gives to others;

that is hidden from us and must remain so, though we are often allowed to see some little fraction of it, so that we may not lose courage. The way in which power works is a mystery."

From the pen of poet Robert Browning: "There is an answer to the passionate longings of the heart for fullness, and I knew it, and the answer is this: Live in all things outside yourself by love, and you will have joy. That is the life of God; it ought to be our life. In him it is accomplished and perfect; but in all created things it is a lesson learned slowly and through difficulty" (qtd. in *Stepping Stones to an Abundant Life*, 119).

From the works of He who has always been willing to serve us: "Do not be discouraged, for I am with you always . . . never weary of good works . . ."

Never. Never. Never.

CHAPTER NINE

Our Author and Our Editor

Relying alone upon the merits of Christ,
who was the author and the finisher of their faith.

—*Moroni 6:4*

Some years ago I got the bright idea to write my family history. No big deal.

Wrong.

It was a very big deal, considering I went back two generations on each side. For starters, my father's Mormon pioneering grandparents each had ten children. In turn, they each had eight children. And those children had children and more children until it was like trying to pedigree all the mice in the pantry.

It took years and the help of hundreds of relatives, mostly a faithful aunt, to get it all sorted out.

"How does the Lord keep track of all of us and our stories?" I asked her.

My aunt is older, much wiser, and much more faithful than I am. "It's not hard for Him," she said, "because Jesus is our author."

The idea intrigued me and I went to a dusty filing cabinet to retrieve an old English handout I had received in college. It is entitled "What a Good Author Does . . ." I would like to share those points with you, keeping in mind that Jesus Christ is not *only* our Author, he is also our Editor, a dual responsibility only He can perform.

A Good Author Reads

We cannot expect to learn a trade unless we study it. If we wish to write young adult fiction, we have to read young adult fiction. Mysteries? Read them. Know the details that makes a piece of writing work. Learn our craft before we attempt to practice it. We do that by writing—"line upon line." We have to be willing to make mistakes if we expect to learn. No author writes a masterpiece the first time her pen touches paper.

Jesus Christ was tutored by Heavenly Father. "In the beginning was the Word, and the Word was with God, and the Word was God. The same was in the beginning with God" (John 1:1–2). "This would indicate that Christ, Jehovah, the Great I Am, was with the Father in that early state of existence; he was the firstborn of his spirit children. He was taught by the Father during that incalculable time" (Joseph Anderson, "A Testimony of Christ," *Ensign*, Nov. 1974, 101).

A GOOD AUTHOR PLANS

The Lord has a good plan for our lives. He knows who we were, who we are, and who we can become. Alma refers to it as "the plan of happiness" (Alma 42:16). "The treasure house of happiness is unlocked to those who live the gospel of Jesus Christ in its purity and simplicity. Like a mariner without stars, like a traveler without a compass, is the person who moves along through life without a plan. The assurance of supreme happiness, the certainty of a successful life here and of exaltation and eternal life hereafter come to those who plan to live their lives in complete harmony with the gospel of Jesus Christ—and then consistently follow the course they have set" (Spencer W. Kimball, *The Miracle of Forgiveness,* 259).

Elder Richard G. Scott says: "Your joy in life depends upon your trust in Heavenly Father and His holy Son, your conviction that their plan of happiness truly can bring you joy" ("Finding Joy in Life," *Ensign*, May 1996, 24).

A GOOD AUTHOR CARES

Our Author cares about each of us. He cares about the details of our lives because he is the Creator. We, of human heart, cannot fathom the depth of His caring. Evidence of His very existence is found in the caring He gives to detail—in the fragile beauty and power of a butterfly's wings, in the folds of a newborn baby's neck, in the ebb and tide of the world's great oceans. "My religion," said Albert Einstein, "consists of a humble admiration of the illimitable superior spirit who reveals himself in the slight details we are able to perceive with our frail and feeble mind."

A Good Author Does Not Stifle His Imagination

The potential within us is limitless. The author and prophet Paul said, "Eye hath not seen, nor ear heard, neither have entered into the heart of man, the things which God hath prepared for them that love him" (1 Cor. 2:9).

A Good Author Knows His Characters

"We are the offspring of God" (Acts 17:29). "All of [us] are children of the most High" (Ps. 82:6). As such, our capabilities are limitless and the Lord will never say, "You've climbed too high," and knock us down. Instead, He will be there beckoning us to climb higher, His steady hand outstretched to lift us to Him.

A teacher once asked me to describe my character's closet.

"What?" I was confused.

A good author knows what clothes hang in his character's closet. How they hang. How his shoes are arranged. What food is in his refrigerator. A good author knows the secrets that his character thinks no one knows. He knows his character's mind and, most importantly, his heart.

A Good Author Is Authentic

"Write what you know about," my first editor admonished. "Otherwise, your work will fall flat. If you want to set your novel in New Orleans, go there, meet the people, eat the food, walk the streets."

Jesus Christ did that. He came to earth, born of a mortal mother, and subjected Himself to all the pains of mortality. "He that ascended up on high, as also he descended below all things, in that he comprehended all things, that he might be in all and through all things, the light of truth" (D&C 88:6).

The sufferings of our Savior were also part of His education. "Though he were a Son, yet learned he obedience by the things which he suffered; And being made perfect, he became the author of eternal salvation unto all them that obey him" (Heb. 5:8–9).

Elder James E. Talmage wrote, "No pang that is suffered by man or woman upon the earth will be without its compensating effect . . . if it be met with patience" (qtd. in Spencer W. Kimball, "Tragedy or Destiny," in *Speeches of the Year, 1955–56,* 5–6).

Jesus is the author of all things authentic. He conducted His research firsthand.

A GOOD AUTHOR APPRECIATES THE POWER OF CONFLICT

Lehi said it best: "For it must needs be, that there is an opposition in all things. If not so . . . righteousness could not be brought to pass, neither wickedness, neither holiness nor misery, neither good nor bad. Wherefore, all things must needs be a compound in one; wherefore, if it should be one body it must needs remain as dead, having no life neither death, nor corruption nor incorruption, happiness nor misery, neither sense nor insensibility" (2 Ne. 2:11).

From the beginning there was good and there was evil. If there is no conflict, there is no growth.

"The life that conquers is the life that moves with a steady resolution and persistence toward a predetermined goal. Those who succeed are those who have thoroughly learned the immense importance of planning in life, and the tragic brevity of time" (W. J. Davison).

In spite of conflict, or ofttimes because of it, the plot of our lives moves forward. "For God is not the author of confusion, but of peace" (1 Cor. 14:33).

Most authors will tell you that every story has three distinct parts. A beginning, a middle, and an end. In the beginning: "We knew the Father of our spirits as well as we know our earthly father here. We knew our elder brother Jehovah and we also knew Lucifer, who too was a son of the morning. We lived by sight at that time. That visual knowledge, the remembrance of that estate, has been taken from our minds, and we are now required to live by faith" (Joseph Anderson, "A Testimony of Christ," *Ensign*, Nov. 1974, 101).

Would mortality be the middle and the end? Well, that's just another beginning in our Author's work.

A GOOD AUTHOR ALLOWS HIS CHARACTERS FREEDOM TO ACT FOR THEMSELVES, TO CHANGE

To be believable a character must be real. The author cannot jump in and manipulate characters or situations. They have to ring true and suffer consequences, be they good or bad.

Behind every action there is a motive; behind every motive there is a reason. And the author, no matter how great the desire to do so, never rescues her characters from the consequences of their actions. Otherwise, there would be no growth.

Orson F. Whitney said, "No pain that we suffer, no trial that we experience is wasted. It ministers to our education, to the development of such qualities as patience, faith, fortitude and humility. All that we suffer and all that we endure, especially when we endure it patiently, builds up our characters, purifies our hearts, expands our souls, and makes us more tender and charitable, more worthy to be called the children of God . . . and it is through sorrow and suffering, toil and tribulation, that we gain the education that we come here to acquire and which will make us more like our Father and Mother in heaven" (qtd. in Kimball, "Tragedy or Destiny," 6).

People are not all evil or all good. They are multi-dimensional. Flat characters are predictable and boring. We are not boring. We have agency to act, consequences to deal with, and the chance to repent. A good author always gives his characters, no matter how dark their situation, hope.

A Good Author Begins with the End in Mind

The gospel of Jesus Christ is an eternal plan and because it is, the Savior's mortal mission, not unlike ours, was divinely designed. The reward for living an obedient life is a sure promise. Whether or not we take our eyes off the mark, the mark remains fixed. Jesus never looked to the right or to the left and we can look to Him. "Looking unto Jesus the author and finisher of our faith; who for the joy that was set before him endured the cross, despising the shame, and is set down at the right hand of the throne of God" (Heb. 12:2).

His reward can be our reward. "We may now be young in our progression—juvenile, even infantile, compared with Him. Nevertheless, in the eternities to come, if we are worthy, we may be like unto Him, enter His presence, 'see as [we] are seen, and know as [we] are known,' and receive a "fullness" (D&C 76:94). (Boyd K. Packer, "The Pattern of Our Parentage," *Ensign*, Nov. 1984, 66).

A Good Author Knows the Finish Is Not the End

Ours is a never-ending story, but resolution is required. Justice and mercy must be served. If we do not finish the work we are given to do, if we do not obey the commandments, if we fall short of the mark, the reward falls from our grasp.

There are no more powerful or poignant words in all of scriptures than those the Savior last spoke to His Author: "The hour is come. . . . I have glorified thee on the earth: I have finished the work which thou gavest me to do" (John 17:1, 4). "Into thy hands I commend my spirit" (Luke 23:46).

Christ's life did not end; it merely opened a new chapter in eternity.

Sisters, every time we truly repent, we are given a clean sheet of crisp, white paper to write our life stories anew. We do it by the words we speak, the acts we perform, the thoughts we entertain. We take what we have gleaned from our pasts to form our futures.

Jesus Christ is the Author of our lives. He is also the Editor, who atoned for our sins so that we might edit out those sins and mistakes that keep us from a joyous ending.

Our lives are not all romance or adventure or mystery. They are a compilation of all types of writing, with the same author holding the pencil—and, thankfully, the eraser.

I know that Jesus Christ lives. He loves each one of us. He cares what happens to us though our stories may not always progress the way we want them to. The actress Gilda Radner understood this concept. "I wanted a perfect ending. Now I've learned, the hard way, that some poems don't rhyme, and some stories don't have a clear beginning, middle, and end. Life is about not knowing, having to change, taking the moment and making the best of it, without knowing what's going to happen next. Delicious Ambiguity."

Ambiguity makes for wonderful adventure. And Faith makes for a wonderful foundation. Elder Jeffrey R. Holland expressed the depth of my sentiment more eloquently than I could ever hope to: He compared life to a play. "We keep on assuming that we know the play. And, in fact, we don't know much about it. We believe we are in Act II, but we know almost nothing of how Act I went or how Act III will be. We are not even sure we know who the major and who the minor characters are. The author knows."

That good Author is Jesus Christ.

Of this I testify.

CHAPTER TEN

Your Worst Day

Behold, the kingdom is yours. And behold, and lo,
I am with the faithful always. Even so. Amen.
—*Doctrine & Covenants 62:9*

It wasn't a safe place to be and I knew it. We were down by the waterfront in a major U.S. city, beneath the viaduct. It hadn't looked so ominous that morning when I had parked the car there. Now that dusk had closed in, long shadows of endless cement pillars, a few cars, but mostly empty parking spaces, made for a horror movie setting.

I sensed it was that dangerous.

"Where did all the people go?" asked my nine-year-old daughter. "This place is deserted."

"Just hurry," I said, pushing the stroller forward. I could see our car but we still had a long way to go before we were safely locked inside.

"I'm tired," my daughter said. "Why did we have to spend the *whole* day shopping?"

"That's what mothers do when they're on vacation," I said. "Now hurry so we can get back to the hotel and rest."

At that moment, from behind the shadows, emerged three very big men dressed in dark, flowing robes. The center man put a filthy boot on the front wheel of the stroller, stopping us in our tracks. His lip curled back into a menacing grin. The man to my left ran a knife blade beneath the dirty crust of his fingernail. The other man eased his way behind us, but not before leaning over to lift the blanket from my sleeping baby.

I clenched the stroller handle with one hand and my daughter's shoulder with the other. I think the imprint of my grip is still indented in her flesh. I've been afraid in my life, but never more terrified than at that moment. How could I keep my children safe?

The center man stepped back and stretched out his arms. "I am the Messiah," he announced.

I knew we were dead. For the first time in my life I had nothing to say.

Not my daughter. She twisted away from me and lifted her chin. "We'll need to see some ID," she told the man.

That was it.

All day long she had been shopping with me, in store after store. As I brought out my credit card, the clerks invariably demanded proof that I was who I claimed to be. "We'll need to see some ID," they'd said.

Now my brave daughter was telling this man who claimed to be the Messiah to prove it.

In only seconds, and without incident, those three men silently retreated back into the shadows, and we raced to the safety of our car.

That experience has had profound influence in my life.

Are we who we claim to be?

Are we?

Jesus Christ said He was the Son of God.

He was.

He is.

Each of our lives is proof of His divine identity, and I promise you with my whole heart and soul that our worst day with Him will be better than our best day without Him.

Think back to your worst day. I've had more than one, but the day that same daughter was hit by a pickup truck has to rank up there at the top. She was struck in the crosswalk on her way home from school. It was a snowy January day and the pickup simply could not stop. My daughter was caught beneath the truck and dragged to the bottom of a hill. Her older sister witnessed the whole thing and ran to tell me. I opened the door and she screamed, "Hurry, Mom! Hurry! She's not dead yet!"

My daughter survived. That does not give comfort to the mothers whose children did not survive accidents or illnesses. My heart goes out to you as does my faith and my love. I cannot know your sorrows or the depth of your despair, but I know One who can and does.

The day my friend Jamie learned that her son had been given the wrong immunization, and the result would be crippling, was her worst day. The day my friend Sylvia learned that her husband had given his heart and body to another woman was her worst day. The day one mother's son was sent home early from his mission was her worst day. The day the cancer came back, the day the doctor said, "Alzheimer's," the day the police showed up at four in the morning, were all listed as "worst days." How grateful I am to have skipped the days when Mormons were driven from their homes and the cities they built, when they witnessed the burning and destruction of their temples. I imagine our pioneer parents could provide an endless list of days that went beyond difficult.

This life is a testing ground. It may seem our trials will never end, but Elder Boyd K. Packer reminds us: "Mortal life is temporary and, measured against eternity, infinitesimally brief. If a microscopic droplet of water should represent the length of mortal life, by comparison all the oceans on earth put together would not even begin to represent everlasting life" ("The Moving of the Water," *Ensign*, May 1991, 7).

Elder Neal A. Maxwell puts his unique spin on the idea that our days, the good, the bad, and the in-between, still add up only to a single day. "One's life . . . is brevity compared to eternity—like being dropped off by a parent for a day at school. But what a day! ("Premortality, a Glorious Reality," *Ensign*, Nov. 1985, 17).

The truth is, no one gets out of this life without their share of painful and pitiful days. No one. "Jesus was not spared grief and pain and anguish and buffeting. No tongue can speak the unutterable burden he carried, nor have we the wisdom to understand the prophet Isaiah's description of him as 'a man of sorrows' (Isa. 53:3). His ship was tossed most of his life, and, at least to mortal eyes, it crashed fatally on the rocky coast of Calvary. We are asked not to look on life with mortal eyes; with spiritual vision we know something quite different was happening upon the cross" (Howard W. Hunter, "Master the Tempest Is Raging," *Ensign*, Nov. 1984, 35).

Joseph had his share of bad days, beginning on a glorious morning when, draped in his father's gift—a coat of many colors—he went to visit his older brothers. "Even before he came near unto them, they conspired against him to slay him" (Gen. 37:18). They cast him in a pit and later sold him to slave traders. Joseph ended up in Egypt where he found favor with Potiphar. He prospered because "the Lord was with [him]," until . . . Potiphar's wife also made Joseph her favorite. When Joseph did the right thing, the moral thing, and rejected her advances, he ended up in prison! Even in prison, "the Lord was with Joseph " (Gen. 39:21), and not for any short duration.

For thirteen years Joseph paid for a crime he did not commit. Joseph's inspiration aided the king's incarcerated baker and butler in getting released. "Please remember me!" Joseph requested, and they swore they would, but the baker was hanged and the butler plain forgot his promise to help free Joseph. Two more years passed; only after Joseph had proven that he would not lose faith, that he would not grow bitter, did the Lord make arrangements for his release. Read chapter 41 of Genesis. Joseph starts out in prison with no hope of parole, but by verse 41, he is ruler over all the land of Egypt.

He progressed from the pit to the palace because he did not permit his bad days to alter his attitude. He remained hopeful and faithful, no matter his circumstances.

We can do the same, but not unless the Lord is with us. Elder Boyd K. Packer explained to those called to shepherd the fold: "It was meant to be that life would be a challenge. To suffer some anxiety, some depression, some disappointment, even some failure is normal. Teach our members that if they have a good, miserable day once in a while, or several in a row, to stand steady and face them. Things will straighten out. There is great purpose in our struggle in life" (*That All May Be Edified,* 94).

Jesus Christ lived thirty-three years in a mortal body. Scripture is sparse on His first thirty years, but it is clear from the record of His final three years that they were filled with plenty of days that could be deemed miserable. Why did He so suffer? Alma prophesied that Christ would "go forth suffering pains and afflictions and temptations of every kind; and this that the word might be fulfilled which saith he will take upon him the pains and the sicknesses of his people. . . . And he will take upon him their infirmities, that his bowels may be filled with mercy, . . . that he may know according to the flesh how to succor his people" (Alma 7:11–12).

Sisters, Christ knows our hearts. He knows the fears they hold, the love they harbor, and the hurt that pounds with every beat. He also knows how to swell our hearts with good tidings and great joy.

In working with women I have discovered that few of us are utterly miserable. Some of us are whiny, some of us are grouchy, some of us are discouraged. All of us are tired. At least from time to time, weariness wears us down until we become susceptible to Satan's cunning lies. We can win that battle in two words: "Look up."

Heber C. Kimball recorded a vision manifested to Joseph Smith that has great significance to every weary woman in this Church. "He saw the Twelve going forth, and they appeared to be in a far distant land. After some time they unexpectedly met together, apparently in great tribulation, their clothes all ragged, and their knees and feet sore. They formed into a circle, and all stood with their eyes fixed upon the ground. The Savior appeared and stood in their midst and wept over them, and wanted to show Himself to them, but they did not discover Him" (Orson F. Whitney, *Life of Heber C. Kimball*, 93; see also *History of the Church*, 2:381).

Joseph the Prophet, at the conclusion of that vision, was privileged to see the completion of the work of the Twelve. Heber C. Kimball records: "He (Joseph) saw until they had accomplished their work, and arrived at the gate of the celestial city; there Father Adam stood and opened the gate to them, and as they entered he embraced them one by one and kissed them. He [Adam] then led them to the throne of God, and then the Savior embraced each one of them and kissed them, and crowned each one of them in the presence of God. . . . The impression this vision left on Brother Joseph's mind was of so acute a nature, that he never could refrain from weeping while rehearsing it"(Whitney, *Life of Heber C. Kimball*, 93–94).

"A message that can be inferred from this is that, because the Twelve had suffered so much, had endured so greatly, and had so exhausted themselves in leading the battle of righteousness, they were bowed down and did not look up. Had they only looked up they might have beheld the Lord Jesus, who wanted them to see him, weeping over them, suffering with them, and standing in their midst" (James E. Faust, "The Dignity of Self," *Ensign*, May 1981, 8).

How many times has the Savior watched over us when we were weary and worn, weeping that we were all alone, when really, if we had looked up we would have known that we are never really alone.

There are times when we feel lost, separated from the fold. It doesn't matter if we were led astray or if we wandered. We still want someone to care enough to come and get us. The two words to win that battle are: Listen up. Listen to the Spirit and obey the Good

Shepherd. He is the one willing to leave the ninety and nine to go in search of the one.

President Boyd K. Packer relates the following event from Church history

> In the late 1850s many converts from Europe were struggling to reach the Great Salt Lake Valley. Many were too poor to afford the open and the covered wagons and had to walk, pushing their meager belongings in handcarts. . . .
>
> One such company was commanded by a Brother McArthur. Archer Walters, an English convert who was with the company, recorded in his diary under July 2, 1856, this sentence:
>
> Brother Parker's little boy, age six, was lost, and the father went back to hunt him (LeRoy R. Hafen and Ann W. Hafen, *Handcarts to Zion,* 61).
>
> The boy, Arthur, was next youngest of four children of Robert and Ann Parker. Three days earlier the company had hurriedly made camp in the face of a sudden thunderstorm. It was then the boy was missed. The parents had thought him to be playing along the way with the other children.
>
> Someone remembered earlier in the day, when they had stopped, that they had seen the little boy settle down to rest under the shade of some brush.
>
> Now most of you have little children and you know how quickly a tired little six-year-old could fall asleep on a sultry summer day and how soundly he could sleep, so that even the noise of the camp moving on might not awaken him.
>
> For two days the company remained, and all of the men searched for him. Then on July 2, with no alternative, the company was ordered west.
>
> Robert Parker, as the diary records, went back alone to search once more for his little son. As he was leaving camp, his wife pinned a bright shawl about his shoulders with words such as these: 'If you find him dead, wrap him in the shawl to bury him. If you find him alive, you could use this as a flag to signal us.'
>
> She, with the other little children, took the handcart and struggled along with the company.
>
> Out on the trail each night Ann Parker kept watch. At sundown on July 5, as they were watching, they saw a figure approaching from the east! Then, in the rays of the setting sun, she saw the glimmer of the bright red shawl.
>
> One of the diaries records: 'Ann Parker fell in a pitiful heap upon the sand, and that night, for the first time in six nights, she slept.'

> Under July 5, Brother Walters recorded: 'Brother Parker came into camp with a little boy that had been lost. Great joy through the camp. The mother's joy I cannot describe' (Hafen and Hafen, *Handcarts to Zion*, 61).
>
> We do not know all of the details. A nameless woodsman—I've often wondered how unlikely it was that a woodsman should be there—found the little boy and described him as being sick with illness and with terror, and he cared for him until his father found him.
>
> So here a story, commonplace in its day, ends—except for a question. How would you, in Ann Parker's place, feel toward the nameless woodsman had he saved your little son? Would there be any end to your gratitude? ("Where Much Is Given, Much Is Required," *Ensign*, Nov. 1974, 88–89).

We are the children of God. The Savior of humanity is our Savior. He atoned because He knew that without His sacrifice, we would lose our way and never make it back home to Father again.

He knew Arthur Parker. He knew Ann Parker. He knows us. "The Savior's Atonement in the garden and on the cross is intimate as well as infinite. Infinite in that it spans the eternities. Intimate in that the Savior felt each person's pains, sufferings, and sicknesses" (Merrill J. Bateman, "The Power to Heal from Within," *Ensign*, May 1995, 13).

"Life is an obstacle course and as we navigate our way through the danger zones, it is inevitable that we stumble and fall, that we sustain injuries. No matter how ideal it sounds for us to get through this life without getting hurt, suffering no battle scars, that is not the plan for which we voted. What we must remember is that Jesus can heal us everywhere we hurt" (Joyce Meyer).

The battle cry against suffering is also only two words: Rise up.

> Now there is at Jerusalem by the sheep market a pool, which is called in the Hebrew tongue Bethesda, having five porches. In these lay a great multitude of impotent folk, of blind, halt, withered, waiting for the moving of the water. For an angel went down at a certain season into the pool, and troubled the water: whosoever then first after the troubling of the water stepped in was made whole of whatsoever disease he had. And a certain man was there, which had an infirmity thirty and eight years. When Jesus saw him lie, and knew that he had been now a long time in that case, he saith unto him, Wilt thou be made whole? The impotent man answered him, Sir, I have no man,

> when the water is troubled, to put me into the pool: but while I am coming, another steppeth down before me. Jesus saith unto him, Rise, take up thy bed, and walk. And immediately the man was made whole, and took up his bed, and walked (John 5:2–9).

It is important to note that Jesus did not ask the lame man if he wanted to walk; he asked him if he wanted to be made whole. To be made whole is to be healed from the inside out.

Presiding Bishop Merrill Bateman noted this fact in the story of the ten lepers. "The Lord said to the one who returned, 'Arise, go thy way: thy faith hath made thee whole' (see Luke 17:12–19). In becoming a whole person, the grateful leper was healed inside as well as on the outside. That day nine lepers were healed skin deep, but only one had the faith to be made whole" (Merrill J. Bateman, "The Power to Heal from Within," *Ensign*, May 1995, 14).

Everything we know of Jesus Christ tells us that He holds a tender place in His perfect heart for the afflicted. He did for the invalid man at Bethesda what the man could not do for himself. I believe He expects all of us to be the angels that trouble the water by helping those less fortunate than we are. But I am still struck by the fact that for thirty-eight years, five years longer than Christ lived, the man stayed poolside, waiting for someone to help him. Even when Christ came by there is no indication that the man asked for help. "When Jesus saw him lie, and knew that he had been now a long time in that case, he saith unto him, Wilt thou be made whole?" The man did not say, "Yes." No, he gave an excuse. Jesus didn't even take him to the water. He simply and lovingly said (to paraphrase) "Get up."

The fact that the man did as he was commanded is indicative of great faith.

Life will knock us down, but instead of crying, "Help, I've fallen and I can't get up," perhaps we should change our plea to, "Help, I've fallen and I can't get up alone." We should do everything we possibly can to get ourselves to the water's edge, to seek help, and to help others once we have been made whole.

President Boyd K. Packer expressed deep concern for those who suffer and those who serve. "I have known some who seemed to enjoy poor health and have interrupted the lives of those who were caring for them unnecessarily, making life miserable for all. They thrive on sympathy, which is generally very low in nourishment. To know just how far to press the handicapped when physical and emotional pain are involved may be the most difficult part for those who serve them. Nevertheless, as the Prophet Joseph Smith said, 'There must be decision of character, aside from sympathy' (*History of the Church*, 4:570)." (Boyd K. Packer, "The Moving of the Water," *Ensign*, May 1991, 19).

There are those who suffer with infirmities that do not allow them to "rise up" on their feet and walk. There are those stricken, only in this life, with bodies and minds that are not whole. I knew one such woman; she was my foster grandmother, Clara Bown. Clara suffered with Parkinson's Disease and could not go outside. She could not drive a car or even make it to the bathroom on her own. Still, I have never met a woman more determined to reach out and lift others. She did that with daily telephone calls to those in need, to encourage, congratulate, or motivate those she knew and loved. Clara wrote notes. When she could no longer write she dictated to others willing to hold the pen for her. But the words were always Clara's. I treasure the notes she sent to me.

There are no easy days, no easy ways. No easy answers. But there is always something more that we can do to make our lives richer—to rise higher, even when our bodies do not let us "rise up." We are spiritual beings; our capabilities are limitless.

Researchers at Baltimore's Johns Hopkins University conducted a study to see if spiritual people are actually able to handle the discomforts and limitations of chronic illnesses better than those who don't consider themselves spiritual. "Previous studies have indicated that people with a strong religious faith or an optimistic personality live longer and get well sooner," reports Reuters. But the Hopkins study wanted to find out if there was a connection between spirituality and the severity of disease. First, the researchers defined spirituality this way: the capacity of an individual to stand outside of his/her immediate sense of time and place and to view life from a larger, more detached perspective. Note that faith is not part of this broad definition. Then they examined 77 rheumatoid arthritis patients, all of whom were thirty or older, and had suffered from the disease for at least two years.

Spirituality did *not* reduce the pain of arthritis, minimize the effects of the disease, or improve mobility. Spirituality *did* help people feel happier and better about their general health (Cathryn Conroy, Netscape News Editor).

We don't need a team of experts to confirm our faith. When we have access to the power of God's holy healing priesthood, when we have access to heaven through prayer, when we have faith unwavering, we can—and should—face every hardship with hope.

Each of us is born into this world as a true individual. One of a kind. What happens to us in our lives—good or bad—helps to shape our personalities. There are those who allow Satan to distract or to halt them altogether. "I'm this way because such-and-such happened to me," we hear.

We may have been neglected or abused but that does not give us the right to neglect or abuse anyone else. We may have been hurt, but our pain does not entitle us to hurt another. The world would have us focus on our wound, medicate it, pick at it until a permanent scar forms. Talk about it endlessly. Not the Lord. He would have us do all we can to heal it, then turn the pain and suffering over to Him, the Master Physician. "Surely he hath borne our griefs, and carried our sorrows: . . . And with his stripes we are healed" (Isa. 53:4–5).

Once we are healed, there is no longer a reason for us to limp through life, not when we walk by faith. There is a wonderful saying oft repeated in Alcoholics Anonymous: "Let go and let God."

Let go of our pain.
Let God heal us.
Let God make us whole.
When we feel tired, may we look up
When we feel lost, may we listen up.
When we feel hurt, may we rise up.

Sisters, I love you. If only you could know my heart you would know these are not merely words on a page. They are feelings seared into my soul. Your worth cannot be measured., but your wounds can be bound up. You can be the whole person God intended you to be.

"In 1977 the Lake Forest College class invited Theodore Geisel, more commonly known as Dr. Seuss, to be its commencement speaker. He approached the podium and announced that he had been researching the function of a commencement address ever since he had been notified of his selection. A speaker, he had found, should give graduates all that he knew of the world's wisdom. Here, in its entirety, is the speech delivered by Dr. Seuss:

My Uncle Terwilliger on the Art of Eating Popovers

My uncle ordered popovers
From the restaurants bill of fare.
And, when they were served,
He regarded them with a penetrating stare . . .
Then he spoke great words of wisdom
As he sat there on the chair:

"To eat these things," said my uncle,
"You must exercise great care.
You may swallow down what's solid . . .
But . . . you must spit out the air!"

And . . . as you partake of the world's bill of fare,
That's darned good advice to follow.
Do a lot of spitting out the hot air
And be careful what you swallow!

"The college's administrators were caught off guard by the brevity of Dr. Seuss's speech, which left a gap in the schedule. To plug up the hole in the program, the dean delivered a 30-minute impromptu speech. We asked several members of the audience what the dean's talk was about, but no one could remember what he had said" (Reprinted from *Chicago Magazine*, September 1977).

When you lay this book aside, I don't suspect you will recall my words, but I pray that you will never forget how you felt as you were reminded of the Savior's promise to you, "Lo, I am with you alway" (Matt. 28:20).

You don't have to be "careful what you swallow" when our Master serves the meal. His words are true and His manna is life eternal. When He stretches out His arms to us and declares, "I am the Messiah," we won't require picture ID from Him; we will know Him as the One who first and best loved us.

In turn, Our Redeemer will know us the same way—by the measure of our hearts.

About the Author

Toni is the author of a number of books, including *Heroes of the Book of Mormon* and *Heroes of the Bible.* She loves the scriptures and children, and tries to embody the best of both loves in her writing.

Toni loves writing, photography, hiking, biking, and people. She and her husband, Ken, and their six children live in Provo, Utah.